BASIC BIBLE DOCTRINES — OF THE CHRISTIAN FAITH

EXPLAINING THE HOLY SPIRIT

Edward D. Andrews

EXPLAINING THE HOLY SPIRIT

Basic Bible Doctrines of the Christian Faith

Edward D. Andrews

Christian Publishing House
Cambridge, Ohio

Christian Publishing House
Professional Christian Publishing of the Good News

Copyright © 2016 Christian Publishing House

All rights reserved. Except for brief quotations in articles, other publications, book reviews, and blogs, no part of this book may be reproduced in any manner without prior written permission from the publisher. For information, write,

support@christianpublishers.org

Unless otherwise stated, scripture quotations are from *The Holy Bible, Updated American Standard Version®*, copyright © 2016 by Christian Publishing House. Used by permission. All rights reserved.

EXPLAINING THE HOLY SPIRIT: Basic Bible Doctrines of the Christian Faith

ISBN-13: 978-0692616338

ISBN-10: 0692616330

Table of Contents

CHAPTER 1 The Spirit and Christians 1

What the Spirit Does for the Christian 10

CHAPTER 2 The Work of the Holy Spirit 20

The Work of the Holy Spirit 33

CHAPTER 3 How Are We to Understand the Indwelling of the Holy Spirit? 36

Jesus Promises the Holy Spirit 43

Paul told the Christians in Rome, ... 45

Paul told the Christians in Colossae, ... 46

Paul told the Christians in Ephesus, ... 48

Bringing This Transformation About 53

CHAPTER 4 The Holy Spirit in the First Century and Today 56

The Need to Be Bold 57

What Was the Reason for the Direct and Supernatural Work of the Holy Spirit in the First Century? 62

What Were the Gifts of the Holy Spirit in the First Century 64

Convicting the World Concerning Sin 66

The Work of the Holy Spirit in the First Century 70

As for Tongues, They Will Cease 70

The Holy Spirit and Today's Christians 83

Obtain Boldness 87

CHAPTER 5 The Spirit and Jesus 92

The Time of Hid Coming Was Clearly Foretold 92

He Was to Come While the Second Temple Was In Existence 92

The Place of His Birth Was Foretold 93

His Lineage Was Declared the In the Hebrew Old Testament 93

The Prophets described his Character 93

His Betrayal and Trial 94

His Resurrection and Coronation 95

He Was Conceived By Holy Spirit 96

He was Anointed By Holy Spirit 96

He Was Led By the Holy Spirit 97

He Performed Miracles By the Holy Spirit 97

He Offered Himself Up Through Holy Spirit 98

He Was Raised By the Holy Spirit 98

He Gave the Commission By the Holy Spirit 98

He Ascended and Coronation Was Announced By the Holy Spirit 99

CHAPTER 6 The Spirit and the Apostles 101

To Convict the World of Sin 106

The righteousness of Jesus Christ 107

Put on the Complete Armor of God 109

CHAPTER 7 The Spirit and the Apostolic Church 111

CHAPTER 8 The Spirit and the World 124

CHAPTER 9 The Parting Word 136

    Blasphemy against the Spirit.............................136

    The Fruit of the Spirit 138

APPENDIX A Is Speaking in Tongues a Biblical Teaching? 142

    What Was the Reason for the Speaking in Tongues? 142

    Modern-day Speaking in Tongues 145

    What is the Real Force Behind Today's Speaking in Tongues? 148

    Should Christians be identified by their ability to "speak in tongues"?...149

    Is this really, what the Bible teaches? 153

    As for Tongues, They Will Cease 154

    Speaking in Tongues and Today's Christianity .155

APPENDIX B Is Snake Handling Biblical? 158

    Founders of Snake Handling 159

    Snake Handlers Today and Practices 159

    Risks of Snake Handling...................................161

Other Books in This Series 171

    The SECOND COMING of CHRIST 171

    What Is Hell?..172

    Where are the Dead? 173

Explaining the Doctrine of Man 174
Bibliography **175**

CHAPTER 1 The Spirit and Christians

By Z. T. Sweeney

Updated[1] By Edward D. Andrews

It has been aptly and truthfully said, "No importance can be attached to a religion that is not begun, carried on and completed by the Spirit of God." That the Christian is led, guided and strengthened by the Spirit cannot be denied by any Bible reader. To deny the fact that the Spirit dwells in us is to deny the Bible. However, it is asserted with equal clearness in the inspired, inerrant Word that *the Father dwells in us*. The apostle Paul wrote, "And what agreement has the temple of God with idols? For we are the temple of the living God; just as God said, '**I will dwell in them** and I will walk among them, and I will be their God, and they shall be my people.'" (2 Cor. 6:16; Lev 26:12; also similar to Jer. 32:38, Eze. 37:27) This not only says that God will dwell in us, but that he *walks in us*. It is also clearly taught that *Christ dwells in us*. Paul wrote, "So that Christ may dwell in your hearts through faith; that you, being rooted and grounded in love." – Ephesians 3:17.

Thus, we see that Scripture clearly teaches that the Father, the Son and the Holy Spirit dwell in us. The question before us is this, is there anything within Scripture that says the Holy Spirit dwells in us in a

---

[1] What do we mean by updated? The chapter's by Sween are from almost one hundred years ago. We update his archaic language and his translation to a modern day translation, such as the UASV, NASB, ESV, HCSB, etc. Nevertheless, what he has to say is very biblical and quite clear.

different *sense* from that in which the Father and the Son dwell in us? The apostle quoted from Leviticus 26:12 in our Scripture above at 2 Corinthians 6:16, where he explained what the Father meant by his words in Leviticus,

2 Corinthians 6:16 Updated American Standard Version (UASV)	Leviticus 26:12 Updated American Standard Version (UASV)
¹⁶ And what agreement has the temple of God with idols? For we are the temple of the living God; just as God said, "I will dwell in them and I will walk among them, and I will be their God, and they shall be my people.	¹² And I will also walk among you and be your God, and you shall be my people.

The Greek word *enoikeso* literally means, "I shall indwell" *en autois* "in them." We learn from Paul's quote of Leviticus 26:12 that God had promised to be in communion with Israel. However, there is nothing in Leviticus 26:12 to show God's personal "indwelling" in any one person.

How does Christ dwell in us? Ephesians 3:17 quoted above says, "Christ may dwell in your hearts through faith;" the Greek literally reading *ho pisteos*, "the faith" or *the gospel*. How does the Spirit dwell in us? Paul asks the Galatians, "Did you receive the Spirit by works of the law or by the hearing of faith?" In other words, 'Did you receive the Spirit by works of the law or by the hearing of the gospel?' The above Scriptures clearly teach that when the words, thoughts, and Spirit of God are controlling in our lives, *God dwells in us*; that when the gospel controls us, *Christ dwells in us*; that when we receive the gospel by the hearing of faith, *the Spirit dwells in us*.

Now, what reason has any man for declaring that the Spirit dwells in us in any other way unless he can point to an explicit declaration of God's word defining and explaining that other way? This cannot be done, for there is no such passage. However, some might argue, "I do not have to depend upon the Word. I know it by my own consciousness." It is a principle as old as metaphysics that consciousness does not take cognizance of causes, but of effects. You may be conscious of an effect within you, but you cannot be aware of the cause that produced the effect.

Suppose you are lying asleep on the ground; a severe pain suddenly awakens you in your lower limb; consciousness tells you that you are suffering pain, but it does not tell you what produced that pain. This must be decided by *reason* or *faith*. If you find a thorn in the grass where your limb was resting, *reason* says the thorn *stuck you*. On the other hand, if you find a bumblebee mashed in the grass, *reason* will say the insect *stung you*; or, if someone near you says, a boy with a pin in his hand ran away from you, *faith* will say the boy *stuck you*.

However, in either case reason or faith decided the cause of your pain. Now, when a man says, "I am conscious of the presence of the Holy Spirit within me," he simply means, "I am conscious of a *feeling* within me which I *have been taught* was caused by the Holy Spirit." If the man has been taught wrong, he assigns a *wrong cause* for the feeling. What is the feeling usually assigned for the presence of the Holy Spirit's personal indwelling?

It is a feeling of joy, peace and love. However, cannot such feeling be excited by other causes?

We know there are dozens of causes that will produce such feelings. In the absence of clear testimony, what right has anyone to attribute such feeling to the personal presence of the Holy Spirit? A man is found murdered. The testimony shows that any one of a dozen men could have killed him. Is there an intelligent jury in the land that would convict anyone of the men of being the murderer? What would you think of a jury that would render such a verdict?

"Well," says one, "what of the great numbers who pray for a 'Pentecostal revival'? Are they all wrong?" Not wrong in what they *want*, but wrong in *what they call it*. All that those people desire, is to be filled with a *genuine revival of religious enthusiasm*. Their mistake is in calling it a "Pentecostal shower." A Pentecostal shower would lead every preacher under its influence to say, with the apostle Peter, to inquiring sinners, "Repent and be baptized every one of you in the name of Jesus Christ for the forgiveness of your sins ..." This is what they are careful *not to say*. It is clear evidence that the Spirit, which guided Peter, is not guiding them. I assert it to be a fact that the Spirit acting through the word of God as clearly accomplishes everything that is claimed to be affected by a personal indwelling of the Spirit.

I do not wish to rest content with asserting that statement, but I wish to prove it. What are the things that might be accomplished by a direct personal indwelling of the Spirit in us?

1. The Holy Spirit might give us faith.

This is accomplished through the Word of God.

Romans 10:17 Updated American Standard Version (UASV)

¹⁷ So faith comes from hearing, and hearing through the word of Christ.

2. The Holy Spirit might enable us to enjoy a new birth.

This is accomplished through the Word of God.

1 Peter 1:23 Updated American Standard Version (UASV)

²³ having been born again, not of perishable seed but of imperishable, through the living and enduring word of God.

3. The Holy Spirit might give us light.

This is accomplished through the Word of God.

Psalm 119:130 Updated American Standard Version (UASV)

¹³⁰ The unfolding of your words gives light; it gives understanding to the simple.

4. The Holy Spirit might give us wisdom.

This is accomplished through the Word of God.

2 Timothy 3:14-15 Updated American Standard Version (UASV)

¹⁴ You, however, continue in the things you have learned and were persuaded to believe, knowing from whom you have learned them, ¹⁵ and that from infancy[2]

---

[2] *Brephos* is "the period of time when one is very young—'childhood (probably implying a time when a child is still nursing), infancy." – GELNTBSD

you have known the sacred writings, which are able to make you wise for salvation through trust[3] in Christ Jesus.

This is accomplished through the Word of God.

Psalm 19:7 Updated American Standard Version (UASV)

⁷ The law of Jehovah is perfect,
restoring the soul;
the testimony of Jehovah is sure,
making wise the simple

5. The Holy Spirit might convert us.

This is accomplished through the Word of God.

Psalm 19:7 Updated American Standard Version (UASV)

⁷ The law of Jehovah is perfect, restoring the soul …

6. The Holy Spirit might open our eyes.

This is accomplished through the Word of God.

Psalm 19:8 Updated American Standard Version (UASV)

⁸ The precepts of Jehovah are right,
rejoicing the heart;
the commandment of Jehovah is pure,
enlightening the eyes.

7. The Holy Spirit might give us understanding.

---

[3] *Pisteuo* is "to believe to the extent of complete trust and reliance—'to believe in, to have confidence in, to have faith in, to trust, faith, trust.' – GELNTBSD

This is accomplished through the Word of God.

Psalm 119:104 Updated American Standard Version (UASV)

104 From your precepts I get understanding;
therefore I hate every false way.

8. The Holy Spirit might preserve or give us life, i.e., quicken us.

This is accomplished through the Word of God.

Psalm 119:50 Updated American Standard Version (UASV)

50 This is my comfort in my affliction,
that your word has preserved me alive.[4]

9. The Holy Spirit might save us.

This is accomplished through the Word of God.

James 1:21 Updated American Standard Version (UASV)

21 Therefore, putting aside all filthiness and abundance of wickedness, and receive with meekness the implanted word, which is able to save your souls.[5]

10. The Holy Spirit might sanctify us.

This is accomplished through the Word of God.

John 17:17 Updated American Standard Version (UASV)

17 Sanctify them in the truth; your word is truth.

---

[4] Older translations read, *quickened me*

[5] Or "is able to save *you*"

11. The Holy Spirit might purify us.

This is accomplished through the Word of God.

"Seeing ye have purified your souls in your obedience to *the truth*

1 Peter 1:22 Updated American Standard Version (UASV)

²² The souls of you having been purified by obedience to the truth, for an unhypocritical love of the brothers, intensely love one another from the heart,[6]

12. The Holy Spirit might cleanse us.

This is accomplished through the Word of God.

John 15:3 Updated American Standard Version (UASV)

³ Already ye are clean because of the word which I have spoken unto you.

13. The Holy Spirit might make us free from sin.

This is accomplished through the Word of God.

Romans 6:17-18 Updated American Standard Version (ASV)

¹⁷ But thanks be to God that you were slaves of sin, but you became obedient from the heart to that form of teaching to which you were committed, ¹⁸ and having been freed from sin, you became slaves of righteousness.

14. The Holy Spirit might impart a divine nature.

---

[6] Two early mss read *a clean heart*

This is accomplished through the Word of God.

2 Peter 1:4 Updated American Standard Version (UASV)

⁴ By which he has granted to us his precious and very great promises, so that through them you may become partakers of the divine nature, having escaped from the corruption that is in the world because of sinful desire.

15. The Holy Spirit might fit us for glory.

This is accomplished through the Word of God.

Acts 20:32 Updated American Standard Version (UASV)

³² And now I commend you to God and to the word of his grace, which is able to build you up and to give you the inheritance among all those who are sanctified.

16. The Holy Spirit might strengthen us.

This is accomplished through the Word of God.

Psalm 119:28 Updated American Standard Version (ASV)

²⁸ My soul weeps[7] because of grief;
strengthen me according to your word!

In the above cases, we have covered all the possible things a direct indwelling Spirit could do for one, and have shown that all these things the Spirit does through the word of God. It is not claimed that a direct indwelling of the Spirit makes any new revelations, adds

---

[7] Lit *drops*

any new reasons or offers any new motives than are found in the word of God. Of what use, then, would a direct indwelling Spirit be? God makes nothing in vain. We are, therefore, necessarily, led to the conclusion that, in dealing with his children today, God deals with them in the same psychological way that he deals with men in inducing them to become children. This conclusion is strengthened by the utter absence of any test by which we could know the Spirit dwells in us if such were the case.

What the Spirit Does for the Christian

1. *The Holy Spirit is active in our birth.*

John 3:5 Updated American Standard Version (ASV)

⁵ Jesus answered, "Truly, truly I say to you, unless someone is born from water and spirit, he is not able to enter into the kingdom of God.

Here is a distinct statement of radical change, so radical as to be likened to a new birth in order that we may enter the kingdom of God. What is it that is born? Christ says, "A man." However, what is a man? We regard a man as having a mind, heart and a body. There is no perfect man where any of these elements is lacking. If, therefore, a man is born again, he must be born in mind, in heart, and in body. How is this birth accomplished? Let us see what the Word says,

John 1:12-13 Updated American Standard Version (ASV)

¹² On the other hand, as many as received him, he gave authority to them to become children of God, to the *ones* trusting in his name; ¹³ who were born, not of

blood,[8] nor of the will of the flesh, nor of the will of man, but of God.

God gives all things—sometimes directly, sometimes through an agent. The Holy Spirit is the agent, i.e., "Born of water and the Spirit." However, an agent often works through an instrument. What is the instrument? It is the Word of God. "The souls of you having been purified by obedience to the truth, for an unhypocritical love of the brothers, intensely love one another from the heart, having been born again, not of perishable seed but of imperishable, **through the living and enduring word of God**." (1 Pet. 1:22, 23).

How can the word of God accomplish the new birth?

Paul tells us, "**All Scripture is inspired by God** and profitable for teaching, for reproof, for correction, for training in righteousness; so that the man of God may be fully competent, equipped for every good work." (2 Tim. 3:16-17) The apostle Peter tells us, "For no prophecy was ever produced by the will of man, but **men carried along by the Holy Spirit** spoke from God." (2 Pet 1:21) The apostle Paul tells us, "For **the word of God is living and active** and sharper than any two-edged sword, and piercing as far as the division of soul and spirit, of both joints and marrow, and able to judge the thoughts and intentions of the heart." (Hebrews 4:12) The Word of God is inspired, literally God-breathed; as the Bible authors were carried along by Holy Spirit, meaning the words are is living and active. Let us listen in

---

[8] Literally "bloods." This is the only place in the NT that you will find the plural form of blood. It possible that it could refer either to hereditary (that is, blood from one's father and mother) or to the OT blood sacrifice. Neither is necessary for birth into the family of God.

as New Testament Bible scholar Thomas D. Lea writes about Hebrews 4:12,

> This vivid expression of the power of God's message provides the explanation for the strong warning of verse 11. Because God's message is alive, active, sharp, and discerning, those who listen to God's message can enter his rest. Two questions are important in this verse. First, what is **the word of God?** Second, what does this passage say about it?
>
> Although the Bible sometimes refers to Christ as God's Word (John 1:14), the reference here is not speaking of Jesus Christ. Here we have a general reference to God's message to human beings. In the past God had spoken to human beings through dreams, angelic appearances, and miracles. He still can use those methods today, but our primary contact with God is through his written Word, the Bible. God's Word will include any method God uses to communicate with human beings.
>
> This verse contains four statements about God's Word. First, it is **living.** God is a **living** God (Heb. 3:12). His message is dynamic and productive. It causes things to happen. It drives home warnings to the disobedient and promises to the believer. Second, God's Word is **active,** an emphasis virtually identical in meaning with the term **living.** God's Word is not something you passively hear and then ignore. It actively works in our lives, changes us, and sends us into action for God.

Third, God's Word penetrates the **soul and spirit.** To the Hebrew people, the body was a unity. We should not think of dividing the soul from the spirit. God's message is capable of penetrating the impenetrable. It can divide what is indivisible. Fourth, God's message is discerning. **It judges the thoughts and attitudes of the heart.** It passes judgment on our feelings and our thoughts. What we regard as secret and hidden, God brought out for inspection by the discerning power of his Word. (Lea, Holman New Testament Commentary: Vol. 10, Hebrews, James 1999, 72)

George Washington put his spirit into the sentence, "United we stand, divided we fall." As long as the American people are faithful to the above words, the spirit of George Washington will live in them. However, make the same words read, "Divided we stand, united we fall," and the spirit of Washington is removed from them. The only way to take the Spirit of God from the word of God is to add to, take from or transpose the Word so it will not say what the Spirit *said in it*.

"Well," says one, "if we are born of the Spirit operating through the Word, must we not understand all the Word in order that we may be born again?" No, the apostle limits the part of the Word we must understand in verse 25 of this same chapter, "This word is the good news that was preached to you." Let us now endeavor to learn how the gospel, good news produces this change. How is the mind born again! In order to learn this we must understand what is the normal condition of the mind of those who are not reborn spiritually and not repentant (unregenerate). In general, we may say it is in a state of *unbelief*. Now, the proclamation of the great facts of the death, burial and resurrection of Christ according to the Scriptures will break up that condition of unbelief and produce a conviction of the truth of the gospel. When the mind is changed from a state of unbelief to one of hearty belief, the birth of the mind is complete.

However, the mind is only a part of man. The heart must be born again. What is the normal state of the unregenerate heart? It is one of either *indifference* or *hatred*. The latter is the former fully ripened. It is said that Voltaire carried a seal ring upon which were engraved the words, "Crush the wretch," and every time he sealed a letter he impressed his spirit of hatred upon that letter. Now, the gospel sets forth the love of God in Christ and the loveliness of Christ's sacrifice for us in such a manner as to change the indifferent or malignant heart into one of supreme love to Christ. When the heart has thus been changed from hatred to love, it is born again.

However, man has also a body, and upon this spirit cannot act. If the body is to be born again, some element must be used that can act upon the body. Hence, our Savior says, "born of water and the Spirit," because water can act upon the body. Now, the only use of water in the new birth is in the act of baptism. All scholars of note in the religious world agree that Christ's use of water in the new birth has reference to baptism. Paul also speaks of "having our hearts sprinkled clean from an evil conscience and our bodies washed with pure water." (Heb. 10:22) Thus, with mind and heart changed by the Spirit through the gospel, and the body solemnly consecrated to God in baptism, the entire man is born again. This is all accomplished by the Spirit of God working *in and through the gospel*.

2. Another work of the Spirit is to "*bear witness with our spirit that we are children of God, and if children, then heirs.*" (Rom. 8:16) It does not say, "bear witness *to* our spirit," but "*with* our spirit." Many people gauge the witness of the Spirit by feelings within themselves. If they feel good, it is evidence to them of the Spirit's testimony, but they frequently feel bad also; whose testimony is that? The testimony of the Spirit should be clear testimony, and not fluctuating; it should be in words, and not in feelings. Feelings, impressions and emotions come and go as the waves of the sea, but words remain forever the same. "Heaven and earth shall pass away, but my word shall not pass away," said the Lord. The idea of the conscious testimony of the Spirit is not sustained by either the Word of God or a correct psychology. It is the testimony of metaphysicians, from Sir William Hamilton down to the writer, that consciousness does not take cognizance of causes, but effects. Feelings are effects and not causes. Consciousness tells us when we feel good or bad, but it does not tell us what makes us feel good or bad. When a man has been taught that a certain feeling in the heart is produced by a certain agency, his faith and reason may decide that that agency produced the feeling, but consciousness has nothing whatever to do with *the cause* of the feeling. Likewise, a certain feeling in the heart may be attributed to the Spirit because one has been taught that the Spirit will produce such a feeling, but consciousness cannot trace that feeling to the Spirit himself. A man should feel right because he knows he is right, and not know he is right because he feels right.

In deciding whether we be children of God, we have two witnesses: first, the Spirit himself, and, second, our spirit. The Spirit testifies as to who is a child of God; our spirits testify as to what we are. If our spirits testify that we are the character, which the Spirit says belongs to a child of God, then we have the testimony of the Spirit himself bearing witness with our spirits that we are children of God. The testimony of the Spirit, in the nature of the case, must be general. He testifies that whosoever believes in Christ, repents of his sins, and is baptized into him, is a child of God. This is the whole of his testimony. Your spirit, likewise, must bear witness to your position on all of these points.

No one but your own spirit can testify that you believe in Christ; you may profess to, and the whole world may believe that you do, but your own spirit knows that you are a hypocrite in making the profession. Likewise, no one can testify but your own spirit that you have repented; you may make professions of repentance, and the world may believe you thoroughly sincere, but your own spirit may tell you that your profession is false. In a similar manner, no one but your own spirit can testify that you have been baptized; your father and mother may say so, the church record may so testify, and yet it is possible for them to be mistaken. To be certain you are a child of God you must have the testimony of your own spirit that you believe, that you have repented and that you have been baptized. If, in the judgment day, God should ask such people, "Have you obeyed me in the act of Christian baptism?" they would not have the testimony of their spirit that they had so obeyed; they would have to fall back upon the church record or that of their father and mother. Others may be satisfied with such testimony, but, as for myself, if I did not have the testimony of my own spirit that I had obeyed the Lord in Christian baptism, I would obtain that testimony before the going down of the sun.

"Well," says one "is that all the witness of the Spirit mentioned by the apostle?" Yes, that is all; absolutely and unqualifiedly all. What more can you desire? "Well," says another, "I want something more than the mere word; I want to be saved like the thief on the cross." How do you know that the thief on the cross was saved? "Oh, the Bible says he was." True, but that is the testimony of the "mere word;" so you have as much testimony to your own salvation as you have for the salvation of the thief on the cross, and it would be impossible for you to have any more. Suppose the Lord were to come down and take you up bodily and set you down before his throne in heaven, and, in the presence of all the angels and archangels, say to you: "My child, your sins are all forgiven." "Now," says one, "that would be testimony indeed." Yes, it would be testimony, but no more testimony than you have in the word of God now; you would then have only the testimony of the "mere word" of God that you were forgiven. All such criticisms arise out of infidelity as to the truthfulness of God's word.

3. *The Spirit make intercession for us*. This is not a work done neither in us nor upon us, but is something done for us before the throne of God. We cannot dogmatize as to *how* the Spirit maketh intercession, but Paul says he does it "*according to the will of God.*" This is a fact that appeals to *our faith* and not to our Christian *experience*. It "cannot be uttered." We can rest upon it and draw comfort from it as a child draws strength from its mother's breast. We can also draw comfort from the fact that Christ "always lives to make intercession" us, though we have no knowledge as to *how* he does it.

4. Another work of the Spirit is to "*change us from glory to glory.*" "But we all, with unveiled face,

reflecting as a mirror the glory of the Lord, are transformed into the same image from glory to glory, even as from the Lord the Spirit." (2 Cor. 3:18) The figure used here by the apostle is taken from the process of mirror-making among the ancients. They had not the glass mirrors of our day, but a mirror of highly polished metal. A piece of coarse metal would be placed upon a stone and the workmen would begin to polish it. At first, it made no reflection at all, but when polished for a while would give a distorted and perverted reflection; but in the process of polishing, that reflection would grow clearer and clearer, when finally a man could behold his face in it perfectly reflected. And so, the same holds true with us. When taken into the great spiritual laboratory of Christianity we are blocks in the rough, but in the polishing process of the church and spiritual surroundings we begin to reflect the image of our Master, and when we have completed the work, we reflect him as perfectly as an imperfect human being can. Take, for illustration, the brothers Peter and John. At first they were called Boanerges, sons of thunder; they wanted to call down fire from heaven to destroy men who differed from them; but in the great laboratory of the Christian life they grew more and more Christlike, transformed by the Spirit of God, until at last we see the old apostle John at Ephesus, beautified and ennobled, sitting in his chair and lifting up trembling hands, and saying to the young disciples: "Little children, love one another, for love is of God." We see the transforming power of the spiritual atmosphere of the church and the Christian life upon human nature. Christian, with this illustration before you, how can you excuse yourself for keeping out of the spiritual atmosphere of God, for staying away from the communion and the spiritual convocation of

God's people? Is it a burden and a duty to attend the house of God, or is it a pleasure gladly and joyfully anticipated? When you rise on the Lord's Day morning, do you say, "Must I go to church today?" or do you say,

"You may sing of the beauty of mountain and dale, The water of streamlet and the flowers of the Vale, But the place most delightful this earth can afford, Is the place of devotion, the house of the Lord"?

5. The last work of the Spirit, which the Word of God mentions, is *"giving life to our mortal bodies."* "If the Spirit of him who raised Jesus from the dead dwells in you, he who raised Christ Jesus from the dead will also give life to your mortal bodies through his Spirit who dwells in you." (Rom. 8:11) This Spirit, which has ever been with us, watching over us, will never leave us until he raises our bodies from the dead and fashions our vile bodies like unto the glorious body of our Lord. It matters much where we now live; it matters little where and how we die. Our bodies may be buried in the unfathomed caves of ocean; they may lie upon some mountain-peak or be placed in a crowded cemetery of some great city. No stone may mark our resting-place, no friend may be able to find the spot and place a flower of love upon it; but the infinite Spirit of God knows that abiding-place, and from our ashes, he will give life to our bodies and present us faultless before the throne of God.

CHAPTER 2 The Work of the Holy Spirit

Edward D. Andrews

Before we begin unraveling one of the touchiest topics in religious circles, it might be best if we borrow the story from Dr. Robert Stein's book, *A Basic Guide to Interpreting the Bible*:

> Tuesday night arrived. Dan and Charlene had invited several of their neighbors to a Bible study, and now they were wondering if anyone would come. Several people had agreed to come, but others had not committed themselves. At 8:00 P.M., beyond all their wildest hopes, everyone who had been invited arrived. After some introductions and neighborhood chit-chat, they all sat down in the living room. Dan explained that he and his wife would like to read through a book of the Bible and discuss the material with the group. He suggested that the book be a Gospel, and, since Mark was the shortest, he recommended it. Everyone agreed, although several said a bit nervously that they really did not know much about the Bible. Dan reassured them that this was all right, for no one present was a "theologian," and they would work together in trying to understand the Bible.
>
> They then went around the room reading Mark 1:1–15 verse by verse. Because of some of the different translations used (the New International Version, the Revised Standard Version, the King James Version, and

the Living Bible), Dan sought to reassure all present that although the wording of the various translations might be different, they all meant the same thing. After they finished reading the passage, each person was to think of a brief summary to describe what the passage meant. After thinking for a few minutes, they began to share their thoughts.

Sally was the first to speak. "What this passage means to me is that everyone needs to be baptized, and I believe that it should be by immersion." John responded, "That's not what I think it means. I think it means that everyone needs to be baptized by the Holy Spirit." Ralph said somewhat timidly, "I am not exactly sure what I should be doing. Should I try to understand what Jesus and John the Baptist meant, or what the passage means to me?" Dan told him that what was important was what the passage meant to him. Encouraged by this, Ralph replied, "Well, what it means to me is that when you really want to meet God you need to go out in the wilderness just as John the Baptist and Jesus did. Life is too busy and hectic. You have to get away and commune with nature. I have a friend who says that to experience God you have to go out in the woods and get in tune with the rocks."

It was Cory who brought the discussion to an abrupt halt. "The Holy Spirit has shown me," he said, "that this passage means that when a person is baptized in the name of Jesus the Holy Spirit will descend upon him like a dove. This is what is called the baptism of the Spirit." Jan replied meekly, "I don't think that's what the meaning is." Cory, however, reassured her that since the Holy Spirit had given him that meaning it must be correct. Jan did not respond to Cory, but it was obvious she did not agree with what he had said. Dan was uncomfortable about the way things were going and sought to resolve the situation. So he said, "Maybe what we are experiencing is an indication of the richness of the Bible. It can mean so many things!"

But does a text of the Bible mean many things? Can a text mean different, even contradictory things? Is there any control over the meaning of biblical texts? Is interpretation controlled by means of individual revelation given by the Holy Spirit? Do the words and grammar control the meaning of the text? If so, what text are we talking about? Is it a particular English translation such as the King James Version or the New International Version? Why not the New Revised Standard Version or the Living Bible? Or why not a German translation such as the Luther Bible? Or should it be the Greek, Hebrew, and Aramaic texts that best reflect what the original authors, such as Isaiah, Paul, and Luke, wrote? And what about the original authors? How are they related to the meaning of the text?

It is obvious that we cannot read the Bible for long before the question arises as to what the Bible "means" and who or what determines that meaning. Neither can we read the Bible without possessing some purpose in reading. In other words, using more technical terminology, everyone who reads the Bible does so with a "hermeneutical" theory in mind. The issue is not whether one has such a theory but whether one's "hermeneutics" is clear or unclear, adequate or inadequate, correct or incorrect.

2 Corinthians 4:3-4 Updated American Standard Version (UASV)

³ And even if our gospel is **veiled**, it is veiled to those who are perishing. ⁴ In their case the god of this world has **blinded the minds of the unbelievers**,[9] to keep them from seeing the light of the gospel of the glory of Christ, who is the image of God.

2 Corinthians 3:12-18 Updated American Standard Version (UASV)

¹² Therefore having such a hope, we use great boldness in our speech, ¹³ and are not like Moses, who used to put a veil over his face so that the sons of Israel would not look intently at the end of what was fading away. ¹⁴ But their **minds were hardened**; for until this very day at the reading of the old covenant the same veil remains unlifted, because **it is taken away only by means of Christ**. ¹⁵ But to this day whenever Moses is read, a veil lies over their hearts; ¹⁶ but whenever one **turns to the Lord, the veil is taken away**. ¹⁷ ow the

---

[9] By **unbelievers** Paul has in view non-Christians (1 Cor. 6:6; 7:12–15; 10:27; 14:22–24). First, the unbelievers of verse 4 are a subset of those who are perishing in verse 3. In other words, the two are the same. Second, the unbelievers are not persons, who have never heard the truth. No, rather, they are persons who have heard the truth, and have rejected it as foolish rubble. This is how this writer is using the term "unbeliever" as well. Technically, how could one ever truly be an unbeliever if they had never heard and understood the truth, to say they did not believe the truth? Therefore, to be an unbeliever, one needs to hear the truth, understand the truth, and reject that truth (i.e., not believing the truth is just that, the truth).

Lord is the Spirit, and where the Spirit of the Lord is, there is freedom. **18** But we all, with unveiled face, beholding as in a mirror the glory of the Lord, are being transformed into the same image from glory to glory, just as from the Lord, the Spirit.

Let us start by looking at an example of blind minds within Scripture. This was not a case of physical blindness, but mental blindness. There was a Syrian military force coming after Elisha, and God **blinded them mentally**. If it had been physical blindness, then each of them would have to have been led by hand. However, what does the account say?

2 Kings 6:18-20 American Standard Version (ASV)

18 And when they came down to him, Elisha prayed to Jehovah, and said, Please strike this people with blindness. And he struck them with blindness according to the word of Elisha. **19** And Elisha said to them, This is not the way, neither is this the city: follow me, and I will bring you to the man whom you seek. And he led them to Samaria. **20** And it came to pass, when they were come into Samaria, that Elisha said, Jehovah, open the eyes of these men, that they may see. And Jehovah opened their eyes, and they saw; and, behold, they were in the midst of Samaria.

Are we to believe that one man led the entire Syrian military force to Samaria? If they were physically blind, they would have to have all held hands. Were the Syrian military forces not able physically to see the images that were before them? No, rather, it was more of an inability to understand them. This must have been some form of mental blindness, where we see everything that everyone else sees, but something just does not register. Another example can be found in the account about the men of

Sodom. When they were blinded, they did not become distressed, running into each other.

Definitely, Paul is speaking of people, who are not receptive to truth, because their heart is hardened to it, callused, unfeeling. They are not responding, because their figurative heart is opposed. It is as though, God handed them over to Satan, to be mentally blinded from the truth, not because he disliked them per se, but because they had closed their hearts and minds to the Gospel. Thus, no manner of argumentation is likely to bring them back to their senses.

However, at one time Saul (Paul) was one of these. Until he met the risen Jesus on the road to Damascus, he was mentally blind to the truth. He was well aware of what the coming Messiah was to do, but Jesus did none of these things because it was not time. Thus, Paul was blinded by his love for the Law, Jewish tradition, and history. So much so, he was unable to grasp the Gospel. Not to mention, he lived during the days of Jesus ministry, studied under Gamaliel, who was likely there in the area. He could have even been there when Jesus was impressing the Jewish religious leaders, at the age of twelve. Therefore, Saul (Paul) needed a real wake-up call, to get through the veil that blinded him.

Hence, a mentally blind person sees the same information as another, but the truth cannot or will not get down into their heart. I have had the privilege of talking to dozens of small groups of unbelievers, ranging from four people to ten people in my life. I saw this in action. As I spoke to these groups, inevitably, I would see the light going off in the eyes of some (they would be shaking their heads in agreement as I spoke). However, others having a cynical look, a doubting look (they would be shaking their heads in disgust or disapproval), and they eventually walked away. This is not saying that the unbeliever cannot understand the Bible; it is simply that they see no significance in it, as it is foolishness to them.

1 Corinthians 2:14 Updated American Standard Version (UASV)

[14] But the natural man <u>does not accept</u> the things of the Spirit of God, for <u>they are foolishness</u> to him, and <u>he is **not able to understand**[10] them, because they are examined spiritually</u>.

Hundreds of millions of Christians use this verse as support that without the "Holy Spirit," we can fully understand God's Word. They would argue that without the "Spirit" the Bible is nothing more than foolish nonsense to the reader. What we need to do before, arriving at the correct meaning of what Paul meant, is grasp what he meant by his use of the word "understand," as to what is 'foolish.' In short, "the things of the Spirit of God" are the "Spirit" inspired Word of God. The natural man sees the inspired Word of God as foolish, and "he is not able to understand them."

Paul wrote, "But the natural man does not accept the things of the Spirit of God, for they are foolishness to him." What did Paul mean by this statement? Did he mean that if the Bible reader did not have the "Spirit" helping him, he would not be able to grasp the correct meaning of the text? Are we to understand Paul as saying

---

[10] "The Greek word *ginosko* ("to understand") does not mean comprehend intellectually; it means know by experience. The unsaved obviously do not experience God's Word because they do not welcome it. Only the regenerate have the capacity to welcome and experience the Scriptures, by means of the Holy Spirit."— (Zuck 1991, 23)

that without the "Spirit," the Bible and its teachings are beyond our understanding?

We can gain a measure of understanding as to what Paul meant, by observing how he uses the term "foolishness" elsewhere in the very same letter. At 1 Corinthians 3:19, it is used in the following way, "For the wisdom of this world is foolishness with God." This verse helps us to arrive at the use in two stages: (1) the verse states that human wisdom is foolishness with God, (2) and we know that the use of foolishness here does not mean that God cannot understand (or grasp) human wisdom. The use is that He sees human wisdom as 'foolish' and rejects it as such.

Therefore, the term "foolishness" of 1 Corinthians 3:19 is not in reference to not "understanding," but as to one's view of the text, its significance, or better yet, lack of significance, or lack of value. We certainly know that God can understand the wisdom of the world, but condemns it as being 'foolish.' The same holds true of 1 Corinthians 1:20, where the verbal form of foolishness is used, "Has not God made foolish the wisdom of the world?" Thus, we have the term "foolishness" being used before and after 1 Corinthians 2:14, (1:20; 3:19). In all three cases, we are dealing with the significance, the value being attributed to something.

Thus, it seems obvious that we should attribute the same meaning to our text in question, 1 Corinthians 2:14. In other words, the Apostle Paul, by his use of the term "foolishness," is not saying that the unbeliever is unable to understand, to grasp the Word of God. If this were the case, why would we ever share the Word of God, the gospel message with an unbeliever? Unbelievers can understand the Word of God; however, unbelievers see it as foolish, having no value or significance. The resultant meaning of chapters 1-3 of 1 Corinthians is that unbelieving world of mankind can understand the Word of God. However, they view it as foolish (missing value or significance). God, on the other hand, understands the wisdom of the world of mankind, but views it foolish (missing value or significance). Therefore, in both cases, the information is understood or grasped; however, it is rejected because to the party considering it, believes it lacks value or significance.

We pray for the guidance of the Holy Spirit, and our spirit, or mental disposition, needs to be attuned to God and His Spirit through study and application. Now, if our mental disposition is not in tune with the Spirit, we will not come away with the right answer. As Ephesians shows, we can grieve the Spirit.

Ephesians 4:30 Updated American Standard Version (UASV)

³⁰ And do not **grieve the Holy Spirit** of God, by[11] whom you were sealed for the day of redemption.

How do we grieve the Holy Spirit? We do that by acting contrary to its leading through deception, human weaknesses, imperfections, setting our figurative heart on something other than the leading.

Ephesians 1:18 Updated American Standard Version (UASV)

¹⁸ having the **eyes of your heart** enlightened, that you may know what is the hope to which he has called you, what are the riches of the glory of his inheritance in the holy ones,

---

[11] Lit *in*

"Eyes of your heart" is a Hebrew Scripture expression, meaning spiritual insight, to grasp the truth of God's Word. So we could pray for the guidance of God's Spirit, and at the same time, we can explain why there are so many different understandings (many wrong answers), some of which contradict each other. This is because of human imperfection that is diluting some of those interpreters, causing them to lose the Spirit's guidance.

A person sits down to study and prays earnestly for the guidance of Holy Spirit, that his mental disposition be in harmony with God's Word [or simply that his heart be in harmony with . . .], and sets out to study a chapter, an article, something biblical. In the process of that study, he allows himself to be moved, not by a mental disposition in harmony with the Spirit, but by human imperfection, by way of his wrong worldview, his biases, his preunderstanding.[12] A fundamental of grammatical-historical interpretation is that that we are to look for the simple meaning, the essential meaning, the obvious meaning. However, when this one comes to a text that does not say what he wants it to say, he rationalizes until he has the text in harmony with his preunderstanding. In other words, he reads his presuppositions into the text,[13] as opposed to discovering the meaning that was in the text. Even though his Christian conscience was tweaked at the correct meaning, he ignored it, as well as his mental disposition that could have been in harmony with the Spirit, to get the outcome he wanted.

---

[12] Preunderstanding is all of the knowledge and understanding that we possess before we begin the study of the text.

[13] Presupposition is to believe that a particular thing is so before there is any proof of it

In another example, it may be that the text does mean what he wants, but this is only because the translation he is using is full of theological bias, which is **violating** grammar and syntax, or maybe textual criticism rules and principles that arrive at the correct reading. Therefore, when this student takes a deeper look, he discovers that it could very well read another way, and likely should because of the context. He buries that evidence beneath his conscience, and never mentions it when this text comes up in a Bible discussion. In other words, he is grieving the Holy Spirit, and loses it on this particular occasion.

Human imperfection, human weakness, theological bias, preunderstanding, and many other things could dilute the Spirit, or even grieve the Spirit. So that while one may be praying for assistance, he is not getting it or has lost it, because one, some, or all of these things he is doing has grieved the Spirit.

Again, it is not that an unbeliever cannot understand what the Bible means; otherwise, there would be no need to witness to him. Rather, he does not have the spiritual awareness to see the significance of studying Scripture. An unbeliever can look at "the setting in which the Bible books were written and the circumstances involved in the writing," as well as "studying the words and sentences of Scripture in their normal, plain sense," to arrive the meaning of a text. However, without having any spiritual awareness about themselves, they would not see the significance of applying it in their lives. 1 Corinthians 2:14 says, "The natural person does not **accept** [Gr., dechomai] the things of the Spirit of God." Dechomai means, "to welcome, accept or receive." Thus, the unbeliever may very well understand the meaning of a text, but just does not *accept*, *receive* or *welcome* it as truth.

Acts 17:10-11 Updated American Standard Version (UASV)

¹⁰ The brothers immediately sent Paul and Silas away by night to Berea, and when they arrived, they went into the synagogue of the Jews. ¹¹ Now these were more noble-minded than those in Thessalonica, who received the word with all readiness of mind,¹⁴ examining the Scriptures daily to see whether these things were so.

Unlike the natural person, the Bereans accepted, received, or welcomed the Word of God eagerly. Paul said the Thessalonians "received [*dechomai*] the word in much affliction, with the joy of the Holy Spirit." (1 Thess. 1:6) At the beginning of a person's introduction to the good news, he will take in the knowledge of the Scriptures (1 Tim. 2:3-4), which if his heart is receptive, he will begin to apply them in his life, taking off the old person and putting on the new person. (Eph. 4:22-24) Seeing how the Scriptures have begun to alter his life, he will start to have a genuine faith in the things he has learned (Heb. 11:6), repenting of his sins. (Acts 17:30-31) He will turn around his life, and his sins will be blotted out. (Acts 3:19) At some point, he will go to God in prayer, telling the Father that he is dedicating his life to him, to carry out his will and purposes. (Matt. 16:24; 22:37) This regeneration is the Holy Spirit working in his life, giving him a new nature, placing him on the path to salvation.—2 Corinthians 5:17.

A new believer will become "acquainted with the sacred writings, which are able to make [him] wise for salvation through faith in Christ Jesus." (2 Tim. 3:15) As

---

¹⁴ Or with all *eager readiness of mind*. The Greek word *prothumias* means that one is eager, ready, mentally prepared to engage in some activity.

the Bible informs us, the Scriptures are holy and are to be viewed as such. If we are to acquire an accurate or full knowledge, to have the correct mental grasp of the things that we carried out an exegetical analysis on, it must be done with a prayerful and humble heart. It is as Dr. Norman L. Geisler said, "the role of the Holy Spirit, at least in His special work on believers related to Scripture, is in illuminating our understanding of the significance (not the meaning) of the text. The meaning is clear apart from any special work of the Holy Spirit." What level of understanding that we are able to acquire is based on the degree to which we are **not** grieving the Holy Spirit with our worldview, our preunderstanding, our presuppositions, our theological biases. In addition, anyone living in sin will struggle to grasp God's Word as well.

No interpreter is infallible. The only infallibility or inerrancy belonged to the original manuscripts. Each Christian has the right to interpret God's Word, to discover what it means, but this does not guarantee that they will come away with the correct meaning. The Holy Spirit will guide us into and through the truth, by way of our working in behalf of our prayers to have the correct understanding. Our working in harmony with the Holy Spirit means that we buy out the time for a personal study program, not to mention the time to prepare properly and carefully for our Christian meetings. In these studies, do not expect that the Holy Spirit is going to miraculously give us some flash of understanding, but rather understanding will come to us as we set aside our personal biases, worldviews, human imperfections, presuppositions, preunderstanding, opening our mental disposition to the Spirit's leading as we study.

The Work of the Holy Spirit

The following is adopted and adapted from Douglas A. Foster of Abilene Christian University.

Christian Publishing House's understanding of the Holy Spirit is **not** that of the Charismatic groups (the ecstatic and irrational), but rather the calm and rational. The work of the Holy Spirit is inseparably and uniquely linked to the words and ideas of God's inspired and inerrant Word. We see the indwelling of the Holy Spirit as Christians taking the words and ideas of Scripture into our mind and drawing spiritual strength from them. The Spirit moves persons toward salvation, but the Spirit does that, in the same way, any person moves another—by persuasion with words and ideas:

> Now we cannot separate the Spirit and the Word of God, and ascribe so much power to the one and so much to the other; for so did not the Apostles. Whatever the word does, the Spirit does, and whatever the Spirit does in the work of converting, the word does. We neither believe nor teach abstract Spirit nor abstract word, but word and Spirit, Spirit and word. But the Spirit is not promised to any persons outside of Christ. It is promised only to them who believe and obey him.[15]

The Holy Spirit works only through the word in the conversion of sinners. In other words, the Spirit acting through the Word of God can accomplish everything claimed to be affected by a personal indwelling of the Spirit.

---

[15] Alexander Campbell, The Christian System (6th ed.; Cincinnati: Standard, 1850), 64.

Longtime preacher Z. T. (Zachary Taylor) Sweeney, in His book *The Spirit and the Word: A Treatise on the Holy Spirit in the Light of a Rational Interpretation of the Word of God*, writes after examining every Scripture that might be used by advocates of a literal personal indwelling of the Holy Spirit,

> In the above cases, we have covered all the conceivable things a direct indwelling Spirit could do for one, and have also shown that all these things the Spirit does through the word of God. It is not claimed that a direct indwelling of the Spirit makes any new revelations, adds any new reasons or offers any new motives than are found in the word of God. Of what use, then, would a direct indwelling Spirit be? God makes nothing in vain. We are necessarily, therefore, led to the conclusion that, in dealing with his children today, God deals with them in the same psychological way that he deals with men in inducing them to become children. This conclusion is strengthened by the utter absence of any test by which we could know the Spirit dwells in us, if such were the case.[16]

Christian Publishing House is defined by our rejection of Holiness and Pentecostal understandings of the Holy Spirit. The Holy Spirit transforms a person, empowering him through the Word of God, to put on the "new person" required of true Christians, "So, as those who have been chosen of God, holy and beloved, put on a heart of compassion, kindness, humility, gentleness and patience." – Colossians 3:12.

---

[16] Z. T. Sweeney, The Spirit and the Word (Nashville: Gospel Advocate, n.d.), 121–26.

Ephesians 4:20-24 Updated American Standard Version (UASV)

20 But you did not learn Christ in this way, 21 if indeed you have heard him and have been taught in him, just as truth is in Jesus, 22 that you take off, according to your former way of life, the old man, who is being destroyed according to deceitful desires, 23 and to be renewed in the spirit of your minds, 24 and put on the new man,[17] the one created according to the likeness of God in righteousness and loyalty of the truth.

Colossians 3:9-10 Updated American Standard Version (UASV)

9 Do not lie to one another, seeing that you have put off the old man[18] with its practices 10 and have put on the new man[19] who is being renewed through accurate knowledge[20] according to the image of the one who created him,

---

[17] An interpretive translation would have, "put on the new person," because it does mean male or female.

[18] Or *old person*

[19] Or *new person*

[20] See Romans 3:20 ftn.

CHAPTER 3 How Are We to Understand the Indwelling of the Holy Spirit?

Edward D. Andrews

1 Corinthians 3:16 Updated American Standard Version (UASV)

¹⁶ Do you not know that you are a temple of God and that the Spirit of God dwells in you?

Before delving into the phrase, "indwelling of the Holy Spirit, let us consider the **mistaken view** of New Testament scholars Simon J. Kistemaker and William Hendriksen, who wrote,

> The Spirit of God lives within you." The church is holy because God's Spirit dwells in the hearts and lives of the believers. In 6:19 Paul indicates that the Holy Spirit lives in the physical bodies of the believers. But now he tells the Corinthians that the presence of the Spirit is within them and they are the temple of God.
>
> The Corinthians should know that they have received the gift of God's Spirit. Paul had already called attention to the fact that they had not received the spirit of the world but the Spirit of God (2:12). He teaches that Christians are controlled not by sinful human nature but by the Spirit of God, who is dwelling within them (Rom. 8:9).

The behavior—strife, jealousy, immorality, and permissiveness—of the Christians in Corinth was reprehensible. By their conduct the Corinthians were desecrating God's temple and, as Paul writes in another epistle, were grieving the Holy Spirit (Eph. 4:30; compare 1 Thess. 5:19).[21]

First, it must be told that I am almost amazed at how so many Bible scholars say nonsensical things, contradictory things when it comes to the Holy Spirit. Bible Commentators use many verses to say that the Holy Spirit literally,

(1) **dwells in** the individual Christian believers,

(2) having **control over** them,

(3) **enabling them** to live a righteous and faithful life,[22]

(4) with the believer **still being able to sin**, even to the point of grieving the Holy Spirit (Eph. 4:30).

Let us walk through this again, and please take it slow, ponder whether it makes sense, is reasonable, logical, even Scriptural. The Holy Spirit literally dwells in individual believers, controlling them so they can live a righteous and faithful life, yet they can still freely sin, even to the point of grieving the Holy Spirit. Does this mean that the Holy Spirit is not powerful enough to prevent their sinful nature from affecting them? The

---

[21] Simon J. Kistemaker and William Hendriksen, *Exposition of the First Epistle to the Corinthians*, vol. 18, New Testament Commentary (Grand Rapids: Baker Book House, 1953–2001), 117

[22] Millard J. Erickson, *Introducing Christian Doctrine* (Grand Rapids: Baker Book House, 1992), 265–270

commentators say the Holy Spirit now controls the Christian, not their sinful nature. If that were true, it must mean the Holy Spirit is ineffectual and less powerful than their sinful nature of the Christian, because the Christian can still reject the Holy Spirit and sin to the point of grieving the Holy Spirit. If the Holy Spirit is controlling the individual Christian, how is it possible that he still possesses free will?

Let us return to the phrase of "indwelling of the Holy Spirit." Just how often do we find "indwelling" in the Bible? I have looked at over fifty English translations and found it once in the King James Version ad two in an earlier version of the New American Standard Bible. One reference is to sin dwelling within us, and the other reference is to the Holy Spirit dwelling within us.

The Updated American Standard Version removed such usage. We may be asking ourselves since "indwelling" is almost nonexistent in the Scriptures, why the commentaries, Bible encyclopedias, Hebrew and Greek word dictionaries, Bible dictionaries, pastors and Christians using it to such an extent, especially in reference to the Holy Spirit. I say in reference to the Holy Spirit because some scholars refer to the indwelling of Christ and the Word of God.

Before addressing those questions, we must take a look at the Greek word behind 1 Corinthians 3:16 "the Spirit of God **dwells [οἰκέω]** in you." The transliteration of our Greek word is *oikeo*. It means "'to dwell' (from *oikos*, 'a house'), 'to inhabit as one's abode,' is derived from the Sanskrit, *vic*, 'a dwelling place' (the Eng. termination —'wick' is connected). It is used (a) of God as 'dwelling' in light, 1 Tim. 6:16; (b) of the 'indwelling' of the Spirit of God in the believer, Rom. 8:9, 11, or in a church, 1 Cor. 3:16; (c) of the 'indwelling' of sin, Rom. 7:20; (d) of the absence of any good thing in the flesh of the believer, Rom. 7:18; (e) of the 'dwelling' together of those who are married, 1 Cor. 7:12-13."[23]

Thus, for our text, means the Holy Spirit dwelling in true Christians. The TDNT tells us, "Jn.'s μένειν [*menein*] corresponds to Paul's οἰκεῖν [oikein], cf. Jn. 1:33: καταβαῖνον καὶ μένον ἐπ' αὐτόν [descending and remaining upon him]. The new possession of the Spirit is more than ecstatic."[24] What does TDNT mean? It means that John is using *meno* ("to remain," "to stay" or "to abide") in the same way that Paul is using *oikeo* ('to dwell').

When we are considering the Father or the Son alone, and even the Father and the Son together, we are able to have a straightforward conversation. However, when we get to the Holy Spirit we tend to get off into mysterious and mystical thinking. When we think of humans and the words *dwell* and *abide*, both have the sense of where we 'live or reside in a place.'

However, there is another sense of 'where we might stand on something,' 'our position on something.' Thus, in English dwell and abide can be used interchangeably, similarly, just as Paul and John use *meno* "abide" or "remain" and *oikeo* "dwell" similarly. Let us look at the apostle John's use of meno,

---

[23] W. E. Vine, Merrill F. Unger, and William White Jr., *Vine's Complete Expository Dictionary of Old and New Testament Words* (Nashville, TN: T. Nelson, 1996), 180.

[24] Gerhard Kittel, Geoffrey W. Bromiley, and Gerhard Friedrich, eds., *Theological Dictionary of the New Testament* (Grand Rapids, MI: Eerdmans, 1964–)

1 John 4:16 Updated American Standard Version (UASV)

¹⁶ We have come to know and have believed the love which God has for us. God is love, and the one who remains [*meno*] in love remains in God, and God remains [*meno*] in him.

Here we notice that God is the embodiment of "love" and if we **abide in** or **remain in** that love, God then **abides in** or **remain in** us. We do not attach any mysterious or mystical sense to this verse, such as God literally being in us and us being in God. If we suggest that this verse, i.e., God being in us, means his taking control of our lives, does our being in God, also mean we control his life? We would think to suggest such a thing is unreasonable, illogical, nonsensical, and such. Commentator Max Anders in the *Holman New Testament Commentary* says, "This is the test of true Christianity in the letters of John. We must recognize the basic character of God, rooted in love. We must experience that love in our own relationship with God. Others must experience this God kind of love in their relationships with us." (Walls and Anders 1999, 211) Our love for God and man is the motivating factor in what we do and not do as Christians. John is saying that we need to remain in that love if we are to remain in God and God is to remain in us. We may be thinking, well, is it not true that God guides and direct us? Yes, however, this is because we have given our lives over to him.

1 John 2:14 Updated American Standard Version (UASV)

¹⁴ I have written to you, fathers, because you know Him who has been from the beginning. I have written to you, young men, because you are strong,

and the word of God remains [*meno*] in you, and you have overcome the evil one.

Here we see that the Word of God abides or remains in us. Does this mean that the Word of God is literally within our body, controlling us? No, this means that our love for God and our love for his Word is a motivating factor in our walk with God. We are one with the Father as Jesus was and is one with the Father and he is one with us. Listen to the words of Paul in the book of Hebrews,

Hebrews 4:12 Updated American Standard Version (UASV)

12 For the word of God is living and active and sharper than any two-edged sword, and piercing as far as the division of soul and spirit, of both joints and marrow, and able to judge the thoughts and intentions of the heart.

Is the Word of God literally living, and an animate thing? No, it is an inanimate object. Is our Bible literally sharper than a two-edged sword? No, if we decide to stab someone with it, it would look quite silly. Is the Word of God literally able to pierce our joints and marrow? No, again, this would seem ridiculous. If we literally hold the Bible up to our head, is it able to discern our thinking, what we are intending to do? What did Paul mean? The Word of God does these things by our being able to evaluate ourselves by looking into the light of the Scriptures, which helps us to identify the intentions of our heart, i.e., inner person. When we meditatively read God's Word daily and ponder what the author meant, we are taking into our mind, God's thoughts and intentions. When we accept the Bible as the inspired, inerrant Word of God, take its counsel and apply its principles in our lives, it will have an impact on our conscience. The conscience is the moral code that God gave Adam and Eve, our mental power or ability that enables us to reason between what is good and what is bad. (Rom. 9:1) Then, the inner voice within us is not entirely ours, but is also God's Word, empowering us to avoid choosing the wrong path.

1 John 2:24 Updated American Standard Version (UASV)

²⁴ As for you, let that remain [*meno*] in you which you heard from the beginning. If what you heard from the beginning remains [*meno*] in you, you also will remain [*meno*] in the Son and in the Father.

Those who had followed Jesus **from the beginning** of his three and half ministry cleaved to what they had heard about the Father and the Son. Therefore, if the same truths are within our heart, inner person, our mental power or ability, we too can **abide** or **remain** [***meno***] in the Son and the Father. (John 17:3) It is as James said, if we draw close to God, through his Word the Bible, he will draw close to us. (Jam. 4:8) In other words, God becomes a part of us and we a part of him through the Word of God that is "living and active, sharper than any two-edged sword, piercing to the division of soul and of spirit, of joints and of marrow, and discerning the thoughts and intentions of the heart."

In John chapter 14, we see this two-way relationship more closely. Jesus said, "Believe me that I am in the Father and the Father is in me, or else believe on account of the works themselves." **(14:11)** He also said, "In that day you will know that I am in my Father, and you in me, and I in you." **(14:20)** We see that the Father and Son have a close relationship, a relationship that we are invited to join.

All through the above discussion of the Father and the Son, we likely had no problem following the line of thought. However, once we interject the Holy Spirit, it is as though our common sense is thrown out. Christians know that the Father and the Son reside in heaven. They also understand that when we speak of the Word of God, the Father and the Son dwelling in us, it is in reference to our being one with them, our unified relationship, by way of the Word of God. However, when we contemplate the Holy Spirit, it is as though our mental powers shut down, and we enter the realms of the mysterious and mysticism. However, we just understood John **14:11** and **14:20**, i.e., how Jesus is in the Father, the Father in Jesus, and their being in us. So, let us now consider the verses that lie between verse **11** and **20**.

Jesus Promises the Holy Spirit

John 14:16-17 English Standard Version (ESV)

[16] And I will ask the Father, and he will give you another Helper, to be with you forever, [17] eventhe Spirit of truth,whom the world cannot receive, because it neither sees him nor knows him. You know him, for he dwells [*meno*] with you and will be in you.

John 14:15-17 Updated American Standard Version (UASV)

[16] And I will ask the Father, and he will give you another Helper, that he may be with you forever; [17] the Spirit of truth, whom the world cannot receive, because it does not see him or know him, but you know him because he remains [*meno*] with you and will be in you.

Do we not find it a bit disconcerting that, all along when looking at John's writings as to the Son and the Father abiding [*meno*] in one another, in us, and us in them. In those places, the translation rendered *meno* as abiding, but now that the Holy Spirit is mentioned, they render *meno* as "dwell."

Do these verses call for us to; drive off the path of reason, into the realms of mysteriousness and mysticism talk? No, these verses are very similar to our 1 John 2:24 that we dealt with above, but will quote again, "Let what you heard from the beginning **abide [meno]** in you. If what you heard from the beginning **abides [meno]** in you, then you too will **abide [meno]** in the Son and in the Father." In 1 John 2:24, we are told that if the Word of God that we heard from the beginning of being a Christian, **abides [meno]** in us, we will **abide [meno]** in the Son and the Father. In John 14:15-17, if we keep Jesus' commands, the Holy Spirit will **dwell**, actually **abide [meno]** in us. In all of this, the common denominator has been the spirit inspired, fully inerrant Word of God. It is what we are to take into our mind and heart, which will affect change in our person, and enable us to abide or remain in the Father and the Son, and they in us, as well as the Holy Spirit abiding or remaining in us.

The Holy Spirit, through the Spirit inspired, inerrant Word of God is the motivating factor for our taking off the old person and putting on the new person. (Eph. 4:20-24; Col. 3:8-9) It is also the tool used by God so that we can "be transformed by the renewal of your mind, so that you may approve what is the good and well-pleasing and perfect will of God." (Rom. 12:2; See 8:9) *The Theological Dictionary of the New Testament* compares this line of thinking with Paul's reference, at Romans 7:20, to the "sin that dwells within me."

The dwelling of sin in man denotes its dominion over him, its lasting connection with his flesh, and yet also a certain distinction from it. The sin which dwells in me (ἡ οἰκοῦσα ἐν ἐμοὶ ἁμαρτία) is no passing guest, but by its continuous presence becomes the master of the house (cf. Str.-B., III, 239).[25] Paul can speak in just the same way, however, of the lordship of the Spirit. The community knows (οὐκ οἴδατε, a reference to catechetical instruction, 1 C. 3:16) that the Spirit of God dwells in the new man (ἐν ὑμῖν οἰκεῖ, 1 C. 3:16; R. 8:9, 11). This "dwelling" is more than ecstatic rapture or impulsion by a superior power.[26]

How does the Holy Spirit control a Christian? Certainly, some mysterious or mystical feeling does not control him.

Paul told the Christians in Rome,

Romans 12:2 Updated Amercan Standard Version (UASV)

² And do not be conformed to this world, but be transformed by the **renewing of your mind**, so that you may prove what the will of God is, that which is good and acceptable and perfect.

---

[25] Str.-B. H. L. Strack and P. Billerbeck, *Kommentar zum NT aus Talmud und Midrasch*, 1922 ff.

[26] Gerhard Kittel, Geoffrey W. Bromiley, and Gerhard Friedrich, eds., *Theological Dictionary of the New Testament* (Grand Rapids, MI: Eerdmans, 1964–), 135

Just how do we **renew our mind**? This is done by taking in an accurate knowledge of Biblical truth, which enables us to meet God's current standards of righteousness. (Titus 1:1) This Bible knowledge, if applied, will allow us to move our mind in a different direction, by filling the void, after having removed our former sinful practices, with the principles of God's Word, principles that guide our actions, especially ones that guide moral behavior.

Psalm 119:105 Updated Amercan Standard Version (UASV)

105 Your word is a lamp to my feet and a light to my path.

The Biblical truths that lay in between Genesis 1:1 and Revelation 22:21 will transform our way of thinking, which will in return affect our mood and actions and our inner person. It will be as the apostle Paul said to the Ephesians. We need to "to put off your old self, which belongs to your former manner of life and is corrupt through deceitful desires, and to be renewed in the spirit of your minds, and to put on the new self, created after the likeness of God in true righteousness and holiness ..." (Eph. 4:22-24) This force that contributes to our acting or behaving in a certain way, for our best interest is internal.

Paul told the Christians in Colossae,

Colossians 3:9-11 Updated American Standard Version (UASV)

9 Do not lie to one another, seeing that you have put off the old man[27] with its practices 10 and have put on

---

[27] Or *old person*

the new man[28] who is being **renewed through accurate knowledge**[29] according to the image of the one who created him, ¹¹ where there is not Greek and Jew, circumcised and uncircumcised, barbarian, Scythian, slave, free; but Christ is all, and in all.

Science has indeed taken us a long way in our understanding of how the mind works, but it is only a grain of sand on the beach of sand in comparison to what we do not know. We have enough in these basics to understand some fundamental processes. When we open our eyes to the light of a new morning, it is altered into and electrical charge by the time it arrives at the gray matter of our brain's cerebral cortex. As the sound of the morning birds reaches our gray matter, it comes as electrical impulses. The rest of our senses (smell, taste, and touch) arrive as electrical currents in the brain's cortex as well. The white matter of our brain lies within the cortex of gray matter, used as a tool to send electrical messages to other cells in other parts of the gray matter. Thus, when anyone of our five senses detects danger, at the speed of light, a message is sent to the motor section, to prepare us for the needed action of either fight or flight.

Here lies the key to altering our way of thinking. Every single thought, whether it is conscious or subconscious makes an electrical path through the white matter of our brain, with a record of the thought and event. This holds true with our actions as well. If it is a repeated way of thinking or acting, it has no need to form a new path; it only digs a deeper, ingrained, established path.

---

[28] Or *new person*

[29] See Romans 3:20 ftn.

This would explain how a factory worker who has been on the job for some time, gives little thought as he performs his repetitive functions each day; it becomes unthinking, automatic, mechanical. These repeated actions become habitual. There is yet another facet to be considered; the habits, repeated thoughts and actions become simple and effortless to repeat. Any new thoughts and actions are harder to perform, as there needs to be new pathways opened up.

The human baby starts with a blank slate, with a minimal amount of stable paths built in to survive those first few crucial years. As the boy grows into childhood, there is a flood of pathways established, more than all of the internet connections worldwide.

Our five senses are continuously adding to the maze. Ps. 139:14: "I will give thanks to you, for I am fearfully and wonderfully made. . . ." (NASB) So, it could never be overstated as to the importance of the foundational thinking and behavior that should be established in our children from infancy forward.

Paul told the Christians in Ephesus,

Ephesians 4:20-24 Updated American Standard Version (UASV)

[20] But you did not learn Christ in this way, [21] if indeed you have heard him and have been taught in him, just as truth is in Jesus, [22] that you take off, according to your former way of life, the old man, who is being destroyed according to deceitful desires, [23] and to be **renewed in the spirit of your minds**, [24] and put on the

new man,[30] the one created according to the likeness of God in righteousness and loyalty of the truth.

How are we to understand being **renewed in the spirit of our minds**? Christian living is carried out through the study and application of God's Word, in which, our spirit (mental disposition), is in harmony with God's Spirit. Our day-to-day decisions are made with a biblical mind, a biblically guided conscience, and a heart that is motivated by love of God and neighbor. Because we have,

- Received the Word of God,
- treasured up the Word of God,
- have been attentive to the Word of God,
- inclining our heart to understanding the Word of God,
- calling out for insight into the Word of God,
- raising our voice for understanding of the Word of God,
- sought the Word of God like silver,
- have searched for the Word of God like gold,
- we have come to understand the fear of God, and have
- found the very knowledge of God, which now
- leads and directs us daily in our Christian walk.

---

[30] An interpretive translation would have, "put on the new person," because it does mean male or female.

Proverbs 23:7 New King James Version (NKJV)

⁷ For as he thinks in his heart, so is he. "Eat and drink!" he says to you, But his heart is not with you. **[Our thinking affects our emotions, which in turn affects our behavior.]**

Irrational thinking produces irrational feelings, which will produce wrong moods, leading to wrong behavior. It may be difficult for each of us to wrap our mind around it, but we are very good at telling ourselves outright lies and half-truths, repeatedly throughout each day. In fact, some of us are so good at it that it has become our reality and leads to mental distress and bad behaviors.

When we couple our leaning toward wrongdoing with the fact that Satan the devil, who is "the god of this world," (2 Co 4:4) has worked to entice these leanings, the desires of the fallen flesh; we are even further removed from our relationship with our loving heavenly Father. During these 'last days, grievous times' has fallen on us as Satan is working all the more to prevent God's once perfect creation to achieve a righteous standing with God and entertaining the hope of eternal life. – 2 Timothy 3:1-5.

When we enter the pathway of walking with our God, we will certainly come across resistance from three different areas (Our sinful nature, Satan and demons, and the world that caters to our flesh). **Our greatest obstacle** is **ourselves**, because we have inherited imperfection from our first parents Adam and Eve. The Scriptures make it quite clear that we are **mentally bent toward bad**, not good. (Gen 6:5; 8:21, AT) In other words, our natural desire is toward wrong. Prior to sinning, Adam and Eve were perfect, and they had the natural desire of doing good, and to go against that was to go against the grain of their inner person. Scripture also tells us of our inner person, our heart.

Jeremiah 17:9 Updated American Standard Version (UASV)

⁹ The **heart is more deceitful** than all else,
and desperately sick;
who can understand it?

Jeremiah's words should serve as a wake-up call, if we are to be pleasing in the eyes of our heavenly Father, we must focus on our inner person. Maybe we have been a Christian for many years; maybe we have a deep knowledge of Scripture, perhaps we feel that we are spiritually strong, and nothing will stumble us. Nevertheless, our heart can be enticed by secret desires, where he fails to dismiss them; he eventually commits a serious sin.

Our conscious thinking (aware) and subconscious thinking (present in our mind without our being aware of it) originates in the mind. For good, or for bad, our mind follows certain rules of action, which if entertained one will move even further in that direction until they are eventually consumed for good or for bad. In our imperfect state, our bent thinking will lean toward wrong, especially with Satan using his world, with so many forms of entertainment that simply feeds the flesh.

James 1:14-15 Updated American Standard Version (UASV)

¹⁴ But each one is tempted when he is carried away and enticed by his own desire.[31] ¹⁵ Then the desire when it has conceived gives birth to sin, and sin when it is fully grown brings forth death.

---

[31] Or "own *lust*"

1 John 2:16 Updated American Standard Version (UASV)

¹⁶ For all that is in the world, the lust of the flesh and the lust of the eyes and the boastful pride of life, is not from the Father, but is from the world.

Matthew 5:28 Updated American Standard Version (UASV)

²⁸ but I say to you that everyone who looks at a woman with lust[32] for her has already committed adultery with her in his heart.

1 Peter 1:14 Updated American Standard Version (UASV)

¹⁴ As children of obedience,[33] do not be conformed according to the desires you formerly had in your ignorance,

If we do not want to be affected by the world of humankind around us, which is alienated from God, we must again consider the words of the Apostle Paul's. He writes (Rom 12:2) "Do not be conformed to this world, but be transformed by the renewal of your mind that by testing you may discern what is the will of God, what is good and acceptable and perfect." Just how do we do that? This is done by taking in an accurate knowledge of Biblical truth, which enables us to meet God's current standards of righteousness. (Titus 1:1) This Bible knowledge, if applied, will enable us to move our mind in a different direction, by filling the void with the

---

[32] ἐπιθυμία [Epithumia] to strongly desire to have what belongs to someone else and/or to engage in an activity which is morally wrong–'to covet, to lust, evil desires, lust, desire.'– GELNTBSD

[33] I.e., *obedient children*

principles of God's Word, principles that guide our actions, especially ones that guide moral behavior.

Psalm 119:105 Updated American Standard Version (UASV)

¹⁰⁵ Your word is a lamp to my feet and a light to my path.

We have said this before but it bears repeating. The Biblical truths that lay in between Genesis 1:1 and Revelation 22:21 will transform our way of thinking, which will in return affect our mood and actions and our inner person. It will be as the apostle Paul set it out to the Ephesians. We need to "to put off your old self, which belongs to your former manner of life and is corrupt through deceitful desires, and to be renewed in the spirit of your minds, and to put on the new self, created after the likeness of God in true righteousness and holiness ..." (Eph. 4:22-24) This force that contributes to our acting or behaving in a certain way, for our best interest is internal.

Bringing This Transformation About

The mind is the mental ability that we use in a conscious way to garner information and to consider ideas and come to conclusions. Therefore, if we perceive our realities based on the information, which surrounds us, generally speaking, most are inundated in a world that reeks of Satan's influence. This means that our perception, our attitude, thoughts, speech, and conduct are in opposition to God and his Word. Most are in true ignorance to the changing power of God's Word. The apostle Paul helps us to appreciate the depths of those who reflect this world's disposition. He writes,

Ephesians 4:17-19 Updated American Standard Version (UASV)

¹⁷ This, therefore, I say and bear witness to in the Lord, that you no longer walk as the Gentiles [unbelievers] also walk, in the futility of their mind [emptiness, idleness, slugishness, vanity, foolishness, purposelessness], ¹⁸ being darkened in their understanding [mind being the center of human perception], alienated from the life of God, because of the ignorance that is in them, because of the hardness of their heart [hardening as if by calluses, unfeeling]; ¹⁹ who being past feeling gave themselves up to shameless conduct,³⁴ for the practice of every uncleanness with greediness.

Hebrews 4:12 Updated American Standard Version (UASV)

¹² For the word of God is living and active and sharper than any two-edged sword, and piercing as far as the division of soul and spirit, of both joints and marrow, and able to judge the thoughts and intentions of the heart.

By taking in this knowledge of God's Word, we will be altering our way of thinking, which will affect our emotions and behavior, as well as our lives now and for eternity. This Word will influence our minds, making corrections in the way we think. If we are to have the Holy Spirit controlling our lives, we must 'renew our mind' (Rom. 12:2) "which is being renewed in knowledge" (Col. 3:10) of God and his will and purposes. (Matt 7:21-23; See Pro 2:1-6) All of this boils

---

³⁴ Or "loose conduct," "sensuality," "licentiousness" "promiscuity" Greek, *aselgeia*. This phrase refers to acts of conduct that are serious sins. It reveals a shameless condescending arrogance; i.e., disregard or even disdain for authority, laws, and standards.

down to each individual Christian digging into the Scriptures in a meditative way, so he can 'discover the knowledge of God, receiving wisdom; from God's mouth, as well as knowledge and understanding.' (Pro. 2:5-6) As he acquires the mind that is inundated with the Word of God, he must also,

James 1:22-25 Updated American Standard Version (UASV)

[22] But be doers of the word, and not hearers only, deceiving yourselves. [23] For if anyone is a hearer of the word and not a doer, he is like a man who looks intently at his natural face[35] in a mirror.

[24] for he looks at himself and goes away, and immediately forgets what sort of man he was. [25] But he that looks into the perfect law, the law of liberty, and abides by it, being no hearer who forgets but a doer of a work, he will be blessed in his doing.

---

[35] Lit *the face of his birth*

CHAPTER 4 The Holy Spirit in the First Century and Today

Acts 4:31 Updated American Standard Version (UASV)

³¹ And when they had prayed, the place in which they were gathered together was shaken, and **they were all filled with the Holy Spirit** and **began to speak the word of God with boldness**.

Just three days before Jesus was executed, Jesus told his disciples, "And this gospel of the kingdom will be proclaimed in all the inhabited earth[36] as a testimony to all the nations, and then the end will come." (Matt. 24:14) Jesus would speak on this again just before he ascended to heaven; Jesus said to his disciples, "Go therefore and make disciples of all the nations ... teaching them to observe all that I commanded you ..." (Matt 28:19-20) Of course, being curious, they were asking him, "Lord, is it at this time you are restoring the kingdom to Israel?" He said to them, "It is not for you to know times or seasons that the Father has fixed by his own authority. But you will receive power when the Holy Spirit has come upon you; and you will be my witnesses in both Jerusalem and in all Judea and Samaria, and to the extremity of the earth."–Acts 1:6-8

It has been and will be mentioned several times in this publication, Christianity has lost its way in the great commission of proclaiming the good news of the kingdom, teaching biblical truths, and making disciples,

---

[36] Or *in the whole world*

even in the face of centuries of intensified missionary work this is true. It is the mission of Christian Publishing House and this author that the first-century lifesaving work of evangelism is restored, so that, all Christians may play a role in making disciples. Therefore, it is tools like this publication and others by this author and other authors, which will enable any willing Christian to share biblical truths effectively within their family, their community, their workplace or their school, to make disciples. Within this chapter, we will cover how the Holy Spirit can enable us to be bold when we are sharing biblical truths with others.[37]

The Need to Be Bold

One can only imagine the joy of making a disciple for Christ, who, in turn, goes out to make disciples himself. Congregation Evangelists, be it male or female should be very involved in evangelizing their communities and helping the church members play their role at the basic levels of evangelism. There is nothing to say that one church could not have many within, who have the calling of an evangelist, which would and should be cultivated. However, like in the first-century, we in the twenty-first-century have many challenges that get in our way. Generally speaking, few today are eager to hear from God's Word, mostly because the majority have preconceived ideas about it (just a man's book, full of errors and contradictions, and the like), many are of

---

[37] A recommend read THE HOLY SPIRIT AND THE CHRISTIAN How Are We to Understand the Work of and the Indwelling of the Holy Spirit? by Edward D. Andrews

http://www.christianpublishers.org/apps/webstore/products/show/5890475

the same mindset as those who were living the days of Noah. "For as in those days before the flood they were eating and drinking, marrying and giving in marriage, until the day that Noah entered the ark." (Matt. 24:38-39, NASB) Then, the apostle Peter warned,

2 Peter 3:3-4 Updated American Standard Version (UASV)

³ Know this first of all, that in the last days ridiculers will come with their ridicule, following after their own desires, ⁴ and saying: "Where is this promised coming of his? For ever since the fathers fell asleep, all continues just as it was from the beginning of creation."

On these verses, David Walls writes, "**In the last days**" refers to all the days between the first advent of the Messiah and the second advent. Characteristic of that time frame, however long it will be, is the fact that people will make fun of the doctrine of the Second Coming. **Ridiculing** toward Christians is to express derision or scorn about a Christian or Christianity, the Bible, or God. It describes the characteristic attitude of the day toward the Second Coming. False teachers argued that the promise of the Second Coming had been delayed so long that we may safely conclude that it would never happen. As far as they could see, the world was going on just as it always had—people lived and died, but nothing really changed." (Walls and Anders 1996, p. 141) Today, we have false teachers on both sides of the second coming fence: (1) ones that scoff at the idea of Jesus' second coming and (2) those that act as though they are prophets of God, knowing the very day and hour.[38] However, we also have those that from liberal

---

[38] A recommended read WHAT DOES THE BIBLE REALLY SAY ABOUT THE SECOND COMING OF CHRIST? by Edward D. Andrews

and moderate "Christianity" that ridicule, mock and oppose conservative Christianity. All of this, and we have not even gotten to those outside of Christianity, who also ridicule, mock and oppose the Almighty God and his Word, the Bible.

As true Christians, we may face ridicule, mocking and opposition from the governmental officials, the news and entertainment media, other religions, and the agnostics and atheists. However, even more, close to home, it may come from those that our children go to school with, their teachers or it may come from those we work with, even from close family members. All of these people need to be evangelized to if we are to carry out the Great Commission of proclaiming and teaching God's Word, to make disciples for Christ. We need to evangelize those in false forms of "Christianity," the unbelievers and those in either of these categories, who are closer to us.

However, we face yet more challenges that are in our way. One such challenge is our human imperfection, i.e., our human weaknesses, such as shyness and fear of being ridiculed, mocked and opposed. Lastly, our greatest obstacle is our church leaders, who are failing to train us to be effective evangelizers in our communities. James, Jesus' half-brother wrote, "One of you says to them [the poor], 'Go in peace, be warmed and filled," without giving them the things needed for the body, what good is that? So also faith by itself, if it does not have works, is dead." (Jam. 2:16-17, ESV) This principle can be carried over to pastors, elders, priests, ministers, who say to their congregation, "**You** need to share the gospel

---

http://www.christianpublishers.org/apps/webstore/products/show/5383701

in **your** community so that **you** may help build up the church for Christ." All of this pointing the finger at them by using the second person pronoun, "**you**" repeatedly, and these leaders have not even given them the tools to be effective evangelists within their community. What good is that? Therefore, their supposed faith that the evangelism work will be done, but having no works of training such ones, means they have no genuine faith at all, it is dead. If we are to persist in sharing the Word of God, this will require that we have the tools to help us (i.e., this book and others like it), as well as boldness. In this chapter, we will focus on boldness.

Ephesians 6:19-20 Updated American Standard Version (UASV)

[19] and for me, that a word may be given to me at the opening of my mouth **boldly**, to make known the mystery of the gospel, [20] for which I am an ambassador in chains, that I may proclaim it **boldly**, as I ought to speak.

The Greek word, *parresia*, "boldness" in verse 19 has the sense of in boldness "in an evident or publicly known manner–'publicly, in an evident manner, well known.'"[39] The Greek word, *parresiazomai*, "boldly" in verse 19, is a "(derivative of *parresia* 'boldness,' 25.158) to speak openly about something and with complete confidence—'to speak boldly, to speak openly.'"[40] However, this boldness, confidence, courage, fearlessness does not give us a license to be blunt or rude to the ones we speak to,

---

[39] Johannes P. Louw and Eugene Albert Nida, *Greek-English Lexicon of the New Testament: Based on Semantic Domains* (New York: United Bible Societies, 1996), 337.

[40] IBID., 398.

even if their demeanor is such. The apostle said to the Christians in Rome, "Never pay back evil for evil to anyone." (Rom. 12:17; See Col. 4:6, NASB) He went on to say, "If possible, so far as it depends on you, be at peace with all men." (Rom. 12:18, NASB) When we go about our evangelism work, sharing God's Word with others, we need to be bold in this hostile world, but it needs to be balanced with tact as well, because our objective is not to offend the one we to whom we are witnessing.

To be sure, this sort of boldness calls for personal qualities that involve much effort that needs to be developed over time. We do not just wake up one morning and decide that we are going to be bold from here forward. In addition, we do not just read a couple of Bible verses about being bold, and then, we are all of a sudden able to be bold in our witnessing to others. "But after we [Paul and his companions] had already suffered and been mistreated in Philippi, as you know, **we had the boldness in our God** to speak to you the gospel of God amid much conflict." (1 Thess. 2:2) We today can acquire a similar boldness if we are hesitant, shy or nervous at the idea of speaking to others about the Word of God.

Paul and his traveling companions had boldness, which you can note he said in the above, "we had the boldness in our God." In other words, God removed Paul's fears and gave him boldness (courage). The rulers, elders, and scribes gathered in Jerusalem and commanded Peter and John to no longer witness about Jesus. These Jewish religious leaders had the power of life and death over them. Of course, they could only take their life, not their opportunity at eternal life. However, Peter and John answered them, "Whether it is right in the sight of God to listen to you rather than to God, you must judge, for we cannot but speak of what we have seen and heard." God was well aware of these threats, but he granted his servants to speak his word "*with all boldness.*" Ac 4:5, 19-20, 29, ESV) The Father had provided them with Holy Spirit. What about us; Should we expect that the Holy Spirit under this direct and supernatural control will guide, lead, and direct us in the same bold way.

What Was the Reason for the Direct and Supernatural Work of the Holy Spirit in the First Century?

A significant change was in the offing. The Jews had followed the lead of their religious leaders in the last act of rebellion, resulting in their rejection as his people. The Mosaic Law was being replaced with the law of Christ. This does not mean that no Jew could be received into the newly founded Christian congregation. To the contrary, the next three and half years would be only the Jewish people, which would make up this new way to God. As was the case with Moses, there was to be a sign, miraculous events, which included the speaking in tongues, this as evidence to those, whose heart was receptive to the truth that the Son of God had come, had given his life for them, and ascended back to heaven. Exodus 19:16-19

However, there was much labor to be done. Beginning in 36 C.E., with the conversion of Cornelius, an uncircumcised Gentile, the gospel got underway in its spread to non-Jewish people of every nation. (Acts, chap. 10) In truth, so swiftly did it spread that by about 60 C.E., the apostle Paul could say that the gospel had been "proclaimed in all creation that is under heaven."

(Col. 1:23) Consequently, by the time of the last apostles death (John c. 100 C.E.), Jesus' faithful followers had made disciples all the way through the Roman Empire—in Asia, Europe, and Africa! By 125 C.E., there were over one million Christians.

If we objectively look at the history of first-century Christianity, the three and a half year ministry of Jesus, founding the Christian congregation, the apostles spreading the good news throughout the whole of the Roman Empire, and the Holy Spirit miraculously guiding, leading and showing the apostles the "things to come," reminding them of all that Jesus had said. The apostles and a select few of others, like Paul, Barnabas, Silas, Apollos, Timothy, Titus, Philip, were under direct and supernatural control as they established Christianity in the first century. While there may have been a few individuals, attempting to cause division in the first century, by 100 C.E. there was but one Christianity, the one Jesus founded and the apostle grew. The twenty-seven books of the New Testament were to be added to the Old Testament by 200 C.E. The particular work of the Holy Spirit that Jesus spoke of had run its course by the death of the apostle John in 100 C.E., as he was the last apostle. After John, no man has been miraculously guided or directed, in the same manner and way, because that same specific work of the Holy Spirit was no longer needed. The work of the Holy Spirit from the second century forward has been within the inspired, inerrant Word of God. There was no need for the Holy Spirit to operate the same as in the first century because the work of setting up Christianity and completing the Word of God was completed. The work of the Holy Spirit now takes place through the Spirit-inspired Word of God.

What Were the Gifts of the Holy Spirit in the First Century

What miraculous, supernatural gifts were the apostles and a select few workers to receive, to establish first century Christianity? They would receive a helper, comforter, an instructor, a guide, a supporter, i.e., the Holy Spirit.

What did Jesus say about the Holy Spirit, being specifically applied to the apostles and a select few other fellow workers, to accomplish their work of establishing Christianity and completing the Bible? He had much to say on this, as we will discover from the texts below. Italics and underlines are mine.

John 14:15-17 Updated American Standard Version (UASV)

¹⁵ "If you love me, you will keep my commandments. ¹⁶ And I will ask the Father, and he will give you another Helper, that he may be with you forever; ¹⁷ the Spirit of truth, *whom the world cannot receive*, because it does not see him or know him, but you know him because *he dwells with you and will be in you*.

John 14:26 Updated American Standard Version (UASV)

²⁶ But the Helper, the Holy Spirit, whom the Father will send in my name, *that one will teach you all things* and *bring to your remembrance* all that I have said to you.

John 15:26 Updated American Standard Version (UASV)

²⁶ "But when the Helper comes, whom I will send to you from the Father, the Spirit of truth, who proceeds from the Father, *that one will bear <u>witness about me</u>*.

John 16:5-8 Updated American Standard Version (UASV)

⁵ But now I am going to him who sent me, and none of you asks me, 'Where are you going?' ⁶ But because I have said these things to you, sorrow has filled your heart. ⁷ Nevertheless, I tell you the truth: it is to your advantage that I go away; for if I do not go away, the Helper will not come to you; but if I go, I will send him to you. ⁸ And when that one arrives, *he will convict the world concerning sin* and *righteousness* and *judgment*;

John 16:12-15 Updated American Standard Version (UASV)

¹² "I still have many things to say to you, but you cannot bear them now. ¹³ But when that one, the Spirit of truth, comes, *he will <u>guide you</u> into all the truth*; for he will not speak from himself, but whatever he hears, he will speak; and *he will declare to you the <u>things that are to come</u>*. ¹⁴ That one will glorify me, for *he will take what is mine and declare it to you*. ¹⁵ All the things that the Father has are mine; therefore I said that he takes what is mine and will declare it to you.

In the above texts, we have a number of things that the Holy Spirit was to do for the apostles and a select few other fellow workers. While the apostle were not ignorant or illiterate as some commentators suppose, they did not possess training in the Rabbinic study of Scripture, such as the apostle Paul had under Gamaliel.

Luke tells us of an account of Peter and John before the Jewish religious leaders, where he writes,

Acts 4:13 Updated American Standard Version (UASV)

¹³ Now when they saw the boldness of Peter and John, and perceived that they were uneducated and untrained men, **they were astonished**, and they recognized that they had been with Jesus.

All of a sudden, Peter and John, literate fishermen were keeping pace with the Jewish religious leaders, who had training in the Rabbinic study of Scripture. This is the Holy Spirit teaching them, guiding them, instructing them, bringing back to their remembrance all that Jesus had said. Therefore, the apostles and a select few fellow workers needed the Holy Spirit if they were to establish Christianity on the grand scale that it was by the end of the first century and complete the New Testament. There was no way that the apostles alone could have educated themselves to the level of Paul, in such a short period, it was the Holy Spirit, who taught and instructed them miraculously. The Holy Spirit guided them as well. One way was in their writings, as no New Testament author contradicted another; they were all one because there was really one author, God. This is actually true of all forty plus authors of the entire Bible. From the second century forward, this has never repeated. In fact, today we have 41,000 different denominations, all teaching different things on the same doctrines.

Convicting the World Concerning Sin

Nisan 14, 33 C.E., the night of the Passover feast with Jesus, he told the apostles, "When he [the Holy Spirit] comes, he will convict the world concerning sin and righteousness and judgment." (John 16:8, ESV) How did the Holy Spirit do this on Pentecost? The first stage was to baptize the apostle in Holy Spirit, which means that they would have been miraculously endowed with guidance, instruction, teachings, and a remembrance of what Jesus had said. Again, looking at Jesus' words just before his ascension, he said, "for John baptized with water, but you will be baptized with the Holy Spirit not many days from now." (Acts 1:5, ESV) The second stage was the work that these ones would carry out in the first century, namely, putting the world on notice (convicting them concerning their sin and righteousness), which was very similar to what the Mosaic Law had done with the Israelites. Remember the words of the apostle Paul,

Romans 5:20-21 Updated American Standard Version (UASV)

[20] The [Mosaic] Law came in so that the transgression would **increase**; but where sin increased, grace abounded all the more, [21] so that, as sin reigned in death, even so grace would reign through righteousness to eternal life through Jesus Christ our Lord.

How did the Mosaic Law make sin "increase"? From Adam's rebellion to the Mosaic Law, man was well aware of right and wrong because even in imperfection he had a sense of right and wrong. God had given Adam and Eve a conscience, an internal mechanism, to evidence the difference between right and wrong. In their perfection, they were able to sin still because even if a perfect person entertains bad thoughts, it will lead to sin and death. (Jam 1:14-15) Nevertheless, humankind in imperfection has a measure of that conscience that was given to Adam and Eve, meaning they have always had a sense of good and bad. However, the Mosaic Law laid our more explicitly what sin was and the different aspects of it. Therefore, the Mosaic Law caused sin to increase. On this Paul wrote,

Romans 7:7-8 Updated American Standard Version (UASV)

⁷ What shall we say then? Is the Law sin? May it never be! On the contrary, I would not have come to know sin except through the Law; for I would not have known about coveting if the Law had not said, "You shall not covet." ⁸ But sin, taking opportunity through the commandment, produced in me coveting of every kind; for apart from the Law sin *is* dead.

Like the apostle Paul, neither Jewish persons nor us today, would know the full range of sin without the Mosaic Law. Paul gave us the example of coveting. The law exposed the coveting spirit that Paul would never have truly recognized in its fullest sense. This is how Paul could say, "apart from the Law sin *is* dead," specifically, it would not be as recognizable, as exposed, as highlighted. The Law made people more aware of the extent of their sinful nature. We should offer a word of caution, though, the Mosaic Law did not move them toward sin, or make sin more appealing, but rather it exposed sin for what it was. Sin is missing the mark of perfection. Sin is being out of harmony with the Creator, his personality, standards, and ways, which he inculcated in his creation. The Law made it possible to convict more people concerning sin. Now, the apostles, baptized in Holy Spirit were going to take this a step further with the law of Christ. Again, Jesus said to his apostles, "When he [the Holy Spirit] comes, he will convict the world [by way of the apostle workers] concerning sin and righteousness and judgment." (John 16:8, ESV)

What do we mean by 'convicting the world concerning sin'? This is not a reference to sin in general, as though, the Holy Spirit would personally come upon a person who just watched a movie they should not have, or they just told a lie, or they committed any sin. When we feel this inner guilt, a groaning of our inner person, because we know we have just done wrong, this is not the Holy Spirit convicting us of that sin. It is the Holy Spirit working through the Word of God, which convicts us of sin. Sin will cause us to feel guilt, anxiety, insecurity, shame. We get a clearer understanding of this when we consider Paul's words that "the work of the law is written on their hearts, while their conscience also bears witness, and their conflicting thoughts accuse or even excuse them." (Rom 2:15, ESV) In other words, when we fall short of God's standards as they are laid out in Scripture or our God given conscience, we will feel an internal groaning within us, which is our conscience convicting us of wrongdoing.

We are born with the weaker version of the conscience that God had given Adam and Eve. It will prevent most humans from committing the obvious right and wrongs, even if they never read the Word of God their entire life. However, considering that almost all of the teachers and professors in the United States and Especially Europe and Canada, are of a liberal progressive mindset, which is contrary to God's standards, the conscience is greatly weakened by Satan's world. If our conscience is ignored, it will become callused and unfeeling, no longer warning us of our wrongdoing, because it no longer wrongdoing in our heart and mind. On the other hand, if Scripture trains our conscience, it will not allow us to commit the wrongdoing in the first place. Returning to the being made bold by the Holy Spirit, we too can receive the Spirit in our evangelism work, but not in the same way and the same sense as the apostles and their fellow workers.

The Work of the Holy Spirit in the First Century

There was a different level of relationship between fist century Christianity and Christianity over the next 2,000 years. It must be remembered that Christ needed (1) **to train** those that would, (2) **establish Christianity**, and (3) **grow Christianity** to the point that it was **extensive** and **united**. This was needed to withstand the apostasy and false teachers that were to come over the next 2,000 years, who would split Christianity into so many factions, finding the truth and the way of the first century today is nigh impossible. All that Jesus and his apostles were to accomplish took place in a mere one hundred years while also publishing the twenty-seven books of the New Testament that later Christians would bring together as one book. There was a definite need for the Holy Spirit in first century Christianity. Let us look at the gifts of prophesy and speaking in tongues.

As for Tongues, They Will Cease

1 Corinthians 13:8-10 Updated American Standard Version (UASV)

⁸ Love never fails. But if there are gifts of prophecy, they will be done away with; if there are tongues,[41] they will cease;[42] if there is knowledge, it will be done away

---

[41] Namely, miraculous speaking in other languages.

[42] MIRACLES - DO THEY STILL HAPPEN TODAY? God Miraculously Saving People's Lives, Apparitions, Speaking In Tongues, Faith Healing by Edward D. Andrews

http://www.christianpublishers.org/apps/webstore/products/show/5823391

with. ⁹ For we have partial knowledge and we prophesy partially, ¹⁰ but when what is complete comes, what is partial will be done away.

Some may argue that the evidence does not give one any idea of when the gift of tongues was to end. However, they would be mistaken in this case. There are three lines of evidence that present the fact that the gift of tongues would die out shortly after the death of the last apostle, which was the apostle John, who died about 98-100 C.E. **First**, the gift of tongues was always passed on to the person, only by an apostle: either by laying his hands on this one, or at least being present. (Acts 2:4, 14, 17; 10:44-46; 19:6; see also Acts 8:14-18.) **Second**, 1 Corinthians 13:8 informed the Corinthian reader specifically that this gift would "cease." In short, the Greek word for cease [*pausontai*], means to 'peter out,' or 'to die out,' not to be brought to a halt. We will deal with *pausontai* more extensively in a moment. **Third**, both one and two are exactly what happened when we look at the history of this gift of tongues. M'Clintock and Strong's *Cyclopaedia* (Vol. VI, p. 320) says that it is "an uncontested statement that during the first hundred years after the death of the apostles we hear little or nothing of the working of miracles by the early Christians." Therefore, following their passing off the scene and after those who in that way had obtained the gift of tongues breathed their last breath; the gift of tongues should have died out with these ones. (Elwell, 2001, 1207-8) This analysis concurs with the intention of those gifts as acknowledged at Hebrews 2:2-4. In other words, The gifts of the Spirit in the first century, which includes speaking in tongues, was evidence that God had abandoned the 1,600 years of the nation of Israel being the way to God to the Christian congregation.

Daniel B. Wallace in his *Greek Grammar Beyond the Basics* helps us to comprehend better how we are to understand *pausontai* of 1 Corinthians 13:8:

> If the voice of the verb here is significant, then Paul is saying either that tongues will cut themselves off (direct middle) or, more likely, cease of their own accord, i.e., 'die out' without an intervening agent (indirect middle). It may be significant with reference to prophecy and knowledge, Paul used a different verb ([*katargeo*]) and out it in the passive voice. In vv 9-10, the argument continues: 'for we *know* in part and we *prophecy* in part; but when the perfect comes, the partial shall be done away with [*katargethesontai*].' Here again, Paul uses the same passive verb he had used with prophecy and knowledge and he speaks of the verbal counterpart to the nominal 'prophecy' and 'knowledge.' Yet he does not speak about *tongues* being done away 'when the perfect comes.' The implication *may* be that tongues were to have 'died out' on their own *before* the perfect comes. (Wallace 1996, 422)

These abilities were only established by the presence or lying on of hands by the apostles. This coincides with 1 Corinthians 13:8 and the history of these phenomena. Our Greek word for "cease" means that the gift of tongues was to 'die out' over time as the last of those who had received this gift passed off the scene of this earth. This is established by the historical fact that the second century saw just that being evidenced. Today, the Christian is moved by Spirit to speak with his heart and mind, defending and establishing the gospel, and destroying false doctrines, snatching some back from the fire. It is these things, which will give credence to the words of the modern-day Christian congregation: "God is really among you."—1 Corinthians 14:24-25.

The special, supernatural gifts, such as speaking in tongues gave impetus to the evangelism work that needed to be done in the first century, into many different lands throughout the Roman Empire. (Matt 28:19-20; Ac 1:8; 2:1-11) In the first century, the ones who spoke in tongues did so in languages that others could understand. (Ac 2:4, 8) If we look at those who claim to do so today, it is some ecstatic explosion of incomprehensible sounds, which only draws attention to them.

1 Corinthians 12:7-11 Updated American Standard Version (UASV)

7 But the manifestation of the Spirit is given to each one for a beneficial purpose. **8** For to one is given speech of wisdom through the Spirit, to another speech of knowledge according to the same Spirit, **9** to another faith by the same Spirit, to another gifts of healing by that one Spirit, **10** to yet another operations of miraculous powers, to another prophesying, to another the distinguishing of spirits, to another different tongues, and to another interpretation of tongues. **11** But all these operations are performed by the very same Spirit, distributing to each one respectively just as it wills.

What we see here mentioned by Paul, apparently does not take place today in any Christian congregation. He is indicating various direct and supernatural manifestations of the Spirit, which was a direct gift from the Holy Spirit. There was a reason for these miraculous gifts, which Paul mentions in his letter to the Ephesians,

Ephesians 4:11-13 Updated American Standard Version (UASV)

¹¹ And he gave some as apostles, and some as prophets, and some as evangelists, and some as shepherds and teachers, ¹² for the equipping of the holy ones or the work of ministry, to the building up of the body of Christ; ¹³ until we all attain to the unity of the faith, and of the knowledge of the Son of God, to a mature man, to the measure of the stature which belongs to the fullness of Christ.

If we look at the above mention history of the Christian congregation of the first century and what was accomplished, it perfectly fits Paul's reasons here. The reason for the direct gifts of the Holy Spirit was (1) **to train** those that would, (2) **establish Christianity**, and (3) **grow Christianity** to the point that it was **extensive** and **united**. This gift of the Spirit accompanied the baptism of the Spirit on the day of Pentecost. As has been mentioned, the 120 disciples in that upper room grew to become a united, one denomination of Christianity, which numbered over one million all throughout the Roman Empire, after a mere century. Therefore, when Peter promised the gift of the Holy Spirit on the day of Pentecost, it **was <u>not</u>** to be universally given across the whole of Christianity until the return of Jesus Christ, applying to all who obeyed the Word of God. Rather, it was limited to those of the first century. Even so, it was the apostles and a select few fellow workers, who manifested the Holy Spirit in a supernatural way, by being miraculously taught, instructed, guided, and bringing to their remembrance exactly what Jesus taught for three and a half years, and what Jesus meant by the words that he used. Yes, there were a number, in the first century, who were used as apostles [those caring for many congregations], and some as prophets [those proclaiming God's Word], and some as evangelists [a proclaimer of the gospel or good news],[43] and some as shepherds [elders or overseers in the congregation] and teachers [those who teach within the congregation].

Philip the Evangelist

Philip preached the Word of God to the Samaritans in the city of Samaria after the great persecution arose following the death of Stephen.

Acts 8:12-17 Updated American Standard Version (UASV)

¹² But when they believed Philip as he preached good news about the kingdom of God and the name of Jesus Christ, they were baptized, both men and women. ¹³ Simon himself also believed, and after being baptized, he continued with Philip; and he was amazed at seeing the signs and great powerful works taking place.

¹⁴ Now when the apostles in Jerusalem heard that Samaria had received the word of God, they sent them Peter and John, ¹⁵ who came down and prayed for them that they might receive the Holy Spirit. ¹⁶ for he had not yet fallen on any of them, but they had only been

---

[43] Basic Evangelism is planting seeds of truth and watering any seeds that have been planted. [In the basic sense of this word (*euaggelistes*), this would involve all Christians.] In some cases, it may be that one Christian planted the seeds, which were initially rejected, so he was left in a good way because the planter did not try to force the truth down his throat. However, sometime later he faces something in life that moves him to reconsider those seeds, and some other Christian waters what had already been planted. This evangelism can be carried out in all of the methods that are available: informal, house-to-house, street, and the like. What amount of time is invested in the evangelism work is up to each Christian to decide for themselves.

baptized in the name of the Lord Jesus. **¹⁷** Then they laid their hands on them and they received the Holy Spirit.

What do we notice here? We have Philip, a very important and prominent evangelist, who took the good news to Samaria. He preached and baptized the Samaritans. Philip was endowed with Holy Spirit with six other men, who were selected for a special service. "These [seven men] set before the apostles, and they prayed and **laid their hands on them**." (Ac 6:6) We see that Philip was able to perform signs and great miracles. If the gift of the Holy Spirit was to be for all who accepted Jesus and was baptized, why did the Samaritans not receive the Spirit? Philip was not an apostle, meaning he could not confer the gift of the Spirit by laying hands on them, even though he had had hands laid on him, and he could perform signs and great miracles. Therefore, Peter and John were dispatched to Samaria, to lay hands on the Samaritans, so that "they might receive the Holy Spirit." It should be noted that the gifts of the Holy Spirit were **always** conveyed to others by the apostles of Jesus Christ (1) laying on of hands (2) or in their presence.

The Holy Spirit Falls on the Gentile

Cornelius was a Gentile an army officer (centurion, KJV), who commanded 100 soldiers. He was "a devout man" who "feared God with all his household, gave alms generously to the people, and prayed continually to God," "an upright and God-fearing man, who is well spoken of by the whole Jewish nation." About the ninth hour of the day, he saw clearly in a vision an angel of God come in and say to him, "Cornelius." And he stared at him in terror and said, "What is it, Lord?" And he said to him, "Your prayers and your alms have ascended as a memorial before God." The angel also told Cornelius, "send men to Joppa and bring one Simon who is called Peter." (Acts 10:1-22) Again, the gifts of the Holy Spirit were always conveyed to others by the apostles of Jesus Christ (1) laying on of hands (2) or in their presence.

Acts 10:44-48 Updated American Standard Version (UASV)

44 While Peter was still speaking these words, the Holy Spirit fell upon all who heard the word. **45** All the circumcised believers[44] who came with Peter were amazed, because the gift of the Holy Spirit had been poured out on the Gentiles also. **46** For they were hearing them speaking with tongues and magnifying God. Then Peter answered, **47** "Can anyone withhold water for baptizing these people, who have received the Holy Spirit just as we have?" **48** And he commanded them to be baptized in the name of Jesus Christ. Then they asked him to remain for some days.

Disciples at Ephesus

In Acts chapter 19, we find Paul meeting up with certain disciples that had been baptized by the John the Baptist. Paul explained that John was not aware of the full Gospel before his death. Below you will notice that these disciples of John had not even heard of the Holy Spirit, even though John pointed his disciples toward Jesus. Yet again, the gifts of the Holy Spirit were always conveyed to others by the apostles of Jesus Christ (1) laying on of hands (2) or in their presence.

---

[44] I.e., faithful ones

Acts 19:1-7 Updated American Standard Version (UASV)

¹ And it happened that while Apollos was in Corinth, Paul traveled through the inland regions and came to Ephesus and found some disciples. ² And he said to them, "Did you receive the Holy Spirit when you believed?" And they said to him, "But we have not even heard that there is a Holy Spirit!" ³ And he said, "Into what then were you baptized?" And they said, "Into the baptism of John." ⁴ And Paul said, "John baptized with a baptism of repentance, telling the people that they should believe in the one who was to come after him, that is, in Jesus." ⁵ On hearing this, they were baptized in the name of the Lord Jesus. ⁶ And when Paul had laid his hands on them, the Holy Spirit came on them, and they began speaking in tongues and prophesying. ⁷ There were in all about twelve men.

Young Timothy

Here is yet another experience where someone has received the Holy Spirit by an apostle laying hands on him or her. Once more, the gifts of the Holy Spirit were always conveyed to others by the apostles of Jesus Christ (1) laying on of hands (2) or in their presence.

2 Timothy 1:4-7 Updated American Standard Version (UASV)

⁴ longing to see you, even as I recall your tears, so that I may be filled with joy. ⁵ For I am reminded of the sincere faith within you, which first dwelt in your grandmother Lois and your mother Eunice, and I am sure that it is in you as well. ⁶ For this reason I remind you to kindle afresh the gift of God which is in you through the laying on of my hands. ⁷ For God did not give us a spirit

of cowardice, but one of power and of love and of soundness of mind.

Christians In Rome

That the gifts of the Holy Spirit were always conveyed to others by the apostles of Jesus Christ (1) laying on of hands (2) or in their presence was clear. Listen to the praise of Paul to these ones in Rome. He writes, "To all those in Rome who are loved by God and called to be holy ones: 'Grace to you and peace from God our Father and the Lord Jesus Christ. First, I thank my God through Jesus Christ for all of you, because your faith is proclaimed in all the world. For God is my witness, whom I serve with my spirit in the gospel of his Son, that without ceasing I mention you always in my prayers, asking that somehow by God's will I may now at last succeed in coming to you.'" Paul goes on to tell these Christians.

Romans 1:11 Updated American Standard Version (UASV)

[11] For I am longing to see you, that I may impart some spiritual gift to you for you to be strengthened;

Notice that Paul could encourage and counsel them from a distance in the longest letter he had penned. However, it was necessary that he be present to convey gifts of the Spirit by his presence or the laying on of hands.

What have we learned thus far? First, the gift of the Spirit was a miraculous, supernatural gift for helping the first-century believers to be bold, to perform signs and miracles, to speak in foreign languages, to be Jesus' "witnesses in Jerusalem and in all Judea and Samaria, and to the end of the earth." (Ac 1:8) We also notice that the gifts of the Holy Spirit were **always** conveyed to others by the apostles of Jesus Christ (1) laying on of hands (2) or in their presence. Moreover, once the last apostle died, John, in 100 C.E., there was no longer one available to convey the gifts of the Spirit.

Therefore, the Greek word at 1 Corinthians 13:8 for "cease" [pausontai], became a reality in that the gifts that had been given 'petered out,' or 'died out,' namely, they were not brought to a halt, as some were, like prophecy. In other words, they died out as the last ones who were given them died at the beginning of the second century. Second, we can see from the letters of the New Testament authors that in the first century, many of the congregations were filled with members that had the supernatural power of the Spirit. Moreover, when we interpret those letters, this must be a part of the historical setting. Below are a few examples from these letters,

Romans 8:9, 23 Updated American Standard Version (UASV)

⁹ However, you are not in the flesh but in the Spirit, if indeed **the Spirit of God dwells in you**. But if anyone does not have the Spirit of Christ, he does not belong to him. ²³ And not only this, but also we ourselves, having the **first fruits of the Spirit**, even we ourselves groan within ourselves, waiting eagerly for our adoption as sons, the redemption of our body.

Romans 15:30 Updated American Standard Version (UASV)

³⁰ Now I urge you, brothers, through our Lord Jesus Christ and through **the love of the Spirit**, that you exert yourselves with me in prayers to God for me,

2 Corinthians 5:5 Updated American Standard Version (UASV)

⁵ Now the one who prepared us for this very thing is God, who gave us **the Spirit as a down payment** of what is to come.

Ephesians 1:13-14 Updated American Standard Version (UASV)

¹³ In whom also, you having heard the word of truth, the gospel of your salvation, in whom also having trusted, were **sealed with the Holy Spirit** of promise, ¹⁴ who is a down payment of our inheritance for the redemption of the possession, to the praise of his glory.

Ephesians 2:18 Updated American Standard Version (UASV)

¹⁸ for through him we both have our **access in one Spirit** to the Father.

Ephesians 5:18 Updated American Standard Version (UASV)

¹⁸ And do not get drunk with wine, for that is[45] dissipation,[46] but be **filled with the Spirit**,

1 Thessalonians 4:8 Updated American Standard Version (UASV)

⁸ Therefore the one who rejects this is not rejecting man, but God, who also **gives his Holy Spirit to you**.

---

[45] Lit *in which is*

[46] behavior which shows lack of concern or thought for the consequences of an action—'senseless deeds, reckless deeds, recklessness.'—GELNTBSD

Titus 3:5 Updated American Standard Version (UASV)

⁵ he saved us, not by deeds of righteousness that we have done, but because of his mercy, through the **washing** of **regeneration** and **renewal by the Holy Spirit**,

Hebrews 2:4 Updated American Standard Version (UASV)

⁴ God also testifying with them, both by **signs** and **wonders** and by various **miracles** and by **gifts of the Holy Spirit** <u>according to His own will</u>.

James 4:5 Updated American Standard Version (UASV)

⁵ Or do you think that the Scripture speaks to no purpose, "The **spirit that dwells in us** strongly desires to envy"?

1 John 2:20, 27 Updated American Standard Version (UASV)

²⁰ But you have been **anointed by the Holy One**, and you all have knowledge. ²⁷ As for you, the **anointing which you received from him remains in you**, and you have no need for anyone to teach you; but as his anointing teaches you about all things, and is true and is not a lie, and just as it has taught you, you remain in him.

1 John 4:13 Updated American Standard Version (UASV)

¹³ By this we know that we are remaining in him and he in us, because he has given **his Spirit to us**.

The Holy Spirit and Today's Christians

Can The Holy Spirit do the same for us? No, the Holy Spirit cannot, at least not in the same way and the same sense. How, then, can we receive the Holy Spirit, to be instructed, guide, taught, reminded and to be directed in our witnessing to others in our evangelism work? As an aside, the answer will apply to every other facet of our Christian life as well, we just happen to be focusing on the evangelism aspect. Let us look at the thought of the Holy Spirit instructing and teaching Christians. Today we have over 41,000 different denominations, all teaching different doctrinal positions on the same subject matter. If we choose just one denomination, we find that each of the tens of thousands of pastors in the churches does not have to teach the same thing about the same doctrine. Then, let us take and one church within that denominations, and we will find that the church members do not all believe the same thing as their pastor.

Thus, we have all sorts of men teaching different views on every doctrine. Let us look at a few examples, so we can better understand. In dealing with inspiration of God's Word, most church leader teach The Infallibilist View, meaning that they believe the Bible is infallible only on matters of faith, but that it contains many mistakes, errors, and contradictions in matters when it touches on science, history, and geography. On the other hand, few conservative church leaders still teach The Inerrantist View, meaning that they believe the Bible is without error of any kind. On the doctrine of the atonement, some leaders have The Penal Substitution View, meaning that they believe that Christ died in our place. Others have the Christus Victor View, meaning that they believe Christ destroyed Satan and his works. While others have The Moral Government View, meaning that they believe Christ displayed God's wrath against sin. Concerning the doctrine of Sanctification, there are four main views. We have the Lutheran View, meaning sanctification as a declaration by God. We have the Calvinist view, meaning sanctification as holiness in Christ and personal conduct. Then, we have the Keswick View, meaning sanctification as resting-faith in the sufficiency of Christ. In addition, we have the Wesleyan, View, meaning entire sanctification as perfect love. Even these four beliefs on sanctification are not completely accepted because each church leader can tweak it to fit his understanding of things. These doctrines are just the beginning. We could cover The Providence Debate, i.e., the sovereignty of God. We could talk about different foreknowledge beliefs, the divine image differences the different salvation beliefs, the different beliefs about the human constitution, eternal security, the destiny of the evangelized, baptism, charismatic gifts, hellfire, and numerous others.

These differences in the Christian leader's beliefs are often contradictory. Are we to believe that the Holy Spirit one church leader to teach that sinners are destined to enteral torment in hellfire while other leaders teach eternal destruction for the sinners? Are we to believe that the Holy Spirit teaches different church leaders four different views on sanctification? The belief that the Holy Spirit is still carrying out the same work today as what the Father and the Son assigned in the first century, place the Holy Spirit in a very unenviable position, i.e., teaching different views on the same doctrine, some of which are even contradictory. Can we accept that the Holy Spirit teaches different views on all doctrinal positions, even being contradictory? Remember, it was the Holy Spirit, who taught and instructed the apostles miraculously. The Holy Spirit guided them as well. One way was in their writings, as no New Testament author contradicted another, they were all one because there was really one author, God. This is actually true of all forty plus authors of the entire Bible. Thus, we are to believe that the Holy Spirit moved over forty Bible authors miraculously, over a 1,600 year period, to pen sixty-six Bible books, in all of which there is not one contraction, error or mistake, but now the Holy Spirit is teaching different views and contradictory information? We would not say in the church of and leader, who taught contradictory information, so why would we accept that the Holy Spirit would do such a thing. Supposing that churches evangelized their own communities, which they do not, but let us suppose they did. How should an atheist feel if different churches came to his home to witness to him and they told him contradictory views about the same doctrine?

The problem is the belief that the Holy Spirit is carrying out the same work after that work was completed in the first century. Only the apostles and a select few fellow workers received the Holy Spirit in a direct and supernatural way, teaching them, guiding them, instructing them, bringing back to their remembrance all that Jesus had said. The apostle Paul told Timothy, "The things which you have heard from me in the presence of many witnesses, entrust these to faithful men who will be able to teach others also." (2 Tim. 2:2) We all know that Timothy traveled with Paul for 15 years, being taught by Paul (Paul already being extremely educated by Gamaliel), but more importantly, miraculously taught and instructed by the Holy Spirit. This clearly was not the case with Timothy (his being taught and instructed by the Holy Spirit in the same way and to the same extent), as Timothy was taught by

Paul and his study of the Old Testament Scriptures. This text evidences that we are to be taught and instructed by Holy Spirit by way of our study the Holy, Spirit-inspired Scriptures.

If the Holy Spirit were miraculously teaching and instructing Christians today, as took place with the apostles and a select few fellow workers, there would be no need for any sort of Bible study tools, such as Bible dictionaries, encyclopedias, word study dictionaries, commentaries, and the like. Even so, while there are no direct Scriptures to evidence Timothy receiving Holy Spirit in the same way as Paul and the twelve apostles, we know that Holy Spirit led Paul to Timothy on his second missionary tour. We know that Paul saw something in Timothy that brought about a 15-year friendship and bond between the two like no other. Timothy became an extremely valuable co-worker of the apostle Paul, in a time, when the Holy Spirit was building the first-century Christian congregation. Therefore, we cannot discount the possibility that Timothy was guided by the Holy Spirit as Paul had been, maybe not to the same degree, and that he was not taught and instructed in the same way and sense but used more directly by the Holy Spirit than those after the first century, including us today. Let us get back to the apostles for a moment. Let us look at the apostles in the very beginning of Acts, as Jesus tells them,

Acts 1:8 Updated American Standard Version (UASV)

[8] But you will receive power when **the Holy Spirit has come upon you**; and you will be my witnesses in both Jerusalem and in all Judea and Samaria, and to the extremity of the earth."

Earlier, Jesus had told them that he was going away and that he was sending them a helper, the Holy Spirit. Now, he specifically tells them, "You [namely, the apostles] will receive power when the Holy Spirit has come upon you, and you will be my witnesses in Jerusalem and in all Judea and Samaria, and to the end of the earth." Just after Jesus said these things, as they were watching, he ascended back to heaven to be with the Father. Some days later on Sivan 6, 33 C.E., they would receive the power of the Holy Spirit, where there was an outpouring of Holy Spirit. (Acts 2:1-17, 38) If they had already received the Holy Spirit, they would not have needed to call the brothers together to determine who was going to replace Judas as the twelfth apostle. Moreover, "they cast lots for them [Joseph called Barsabbas, who was also called Justus, and Matthias], and the lot fell on Matthias, and he was numbered with the eleven apostles."–Acts 1:15-26

Obtain Boldness

Jesus told his listeners,

Luke 11:13 Updated American Standard Version (UASV)

¹³ If you then, being evil, know how to give good gifts to your children, how much more will your heavenly Father give the Holy Spirit to those who ask Him?"

If we want to receive the Holy Spirit, we just go to the Father in prayer and ask him. If want to be bolder in our sharing of the good news, we can pray to God for the Holy Spirit. However, we must not misunderstand the Scriptures, so as to expect the miraculous, supernatural gifts of the Holy Spirit in the same sense and the same way as the apostle, their fellow workers, and the Christians of the first century. If want to become a better teacher in the Bible class at our churches, we will have to be a better Bible student, take in many Scriptures that deal with the principles of being a more effective teacher, put these into practice, and maybe pick up some good Christian books on being a better teacher. In this way, we would be working in harmony with our prayer, because the Word of God is Spirit inspired, and thus the more we delve into it and apply it in a correct and balanced manner; in essence, we are getting more Holy Spirit. If we want to teach the Bible to the Spanish-speaking people in our community, we may want to learn the Spanish language.

Some might believe that I am suggesting that the Holy Spirit is not active today. This is not the case. It is not the question of whether the Spirit is active, but how the Spirit is active. We can all agree that the Holy Spirit is pleading with the unsaved world, to help them find the path of salvation that leads to accepting Jesus Christ. This is not accomplished in some miraculous, supernatural way, but rather through our work as ambassadors for Christ. New Testament Bible scholar Richard L. Pratt Jr., made the following comment on 1 Corinthians 5:20a,

> Paul's role in the divine plan of reconciliation led him to a remarkable claim. He and his company were **Christ's ambassadors**. "Ambassadors" was a technical political term used in Paul's day that closely parallels our English word "ambassadors." An ambassador represented a nation or kingdom in communication with other nations. Paul had in mind his apostolic call to represent the kingdom of Christ to the nations of the earth. Ambassadors held positions of great honor in

the ancient world because they represented the authority of the kings on whose behalf they spoke.

This was also true for Paul as the ambassador of Christ. When he spoke the message of reconciliation, it was **as though God were making his appeal through** him. Rather than speaking directly to the nations of earth, God ordained that human spokespersons would speak for him. As an apostle, Paul had authority to lead and guide the church (2 Cor. 13:3, 10). Yet, this description applies to all who bear the gospel of Christ to others—even to those who do not bear apostolic authority (1 Pet. 4:11). Though we may not present the gospel as perfectly as Paul did, we do speak on God's behalf when we bring the message of grace to others. But Paul and his company were to be received as mouthpieces of God in the most authoritative sense. (Pratt Jr 2000, p. 359)

2 Corinthians 5:16-20 Updated American Standard Version (UASV)

[16] From now on, therefore, we regard no one according to the flesh. Even though we once regarded Christ according to the flesh, we regard him thus no longer. [17] Therefore if anyone is in Christ, he is a new creation; the old things have passed away; behold, new things have come. [18] And all these things are from God, who has reconciled us to himself through Christ, and who has given us the ministry of reconciliation, [19] namely, that God was in Christ reconciling the world to himself, not counting their trespasses against them, and entrusting to us the message of reconciliation. [20] Therefore, we are

ambassadors for Christ, as though God were making an appeal through us; we beg you on behalf of Christ, be reconciled to God.

As ambassadors for Christ, we are not seeking to offer superficial feel-good solutions to the problems of their imperfection, nor the wicked world in which we live. We are not telling them that, if they accept Christ, God will take care of their problems, and they will feel better about life. Sadly, many who first come to a Christian meeting are looking for just that; they want God to help them cope with the imperfection that surrounds their every waking moment. We certainly can counsel them biblically, which will enable them to improve their lot in life, will help them be stronger in dealing with this imperfection we all face, and, generally speaking, if they live a Christlike life, there will be fewer problems that a worldly life. However, our serving as ambassadors for Christ, this is not the goal of our service to the unbelieving world. We are offering them the same gospel that Paul did. In other words, the Father loved the world of humankind so much, he offered the only begotten Son, and the Father is willing to forgive any of their Adamic, inherited sin, by means of Christ Jesus. Paul wrote,

Romans 5:10-12, 8:32 Updated American Standard Version (UASV)

[10] For if while we were enemies we were reconciled to God through the death of his Son, much more, having been reconciled, we shall be saved by his life. [11] Not only that, but we are also exulting in God through our Lord Jesus Christ, through whom we have now received the reconciliation.

¹² Therefore, just as through one man sin entered into the world, and death through sin, and so death spread to all men, because all sinned,

³² He who did not spare his own Son, but delivered him over for us all, how will he not also with him freely give us all things?

CHAPTER 5 The Spirit and Jesus

By Z. T. Sweeney

Updated By Edward D. Andrews

The relation sustained by the Holy Spirit to Jesus Christ is a twofold one. First: He predicted by the holy prophets the great facts in the life of the coming one. Second: He associated himself with that one after he came.

The Time of Hid Coming Was Clearly Foretold

Isaiah 2:2 Updated American Standard Version (UASV)

² It will come to pass in the latter days
 that the mountain of the house of Jehovah
will be established on the top of the mountains,
 and will be lifted up above the hills;
and all the nations will stream to it,

He Was to Come While the Second Temple Was In Existence

Malachi 3:1 Updated American Standard Version (UASV)

3 "Look! I am going to send my messenger, and he will prepare the way before me. And the Lord whom you are seeking will come suddenly to his temple, and the messenger of the covenant will come, in whom you take delight, behold, he is coming," says Jehovah of hosts.

The Place of His Birth Was Foretold

"But thou, Bethlehem Ephrathah, which art little to be among the thousands of Judah, out of thee shall one come forth unto me that is to be ruler in Israel; whose goings forth are from of old, from everlasting" (Mic. 5:2).

His Lineage Was Declared the In the Hebrew Old Testament

(1) **He was to be a descendant of Abraham**. "I will bless those who bless you, and him who dishonors you I will curse, and in you all the families of the earth shall be blessed." (Gen. 12:3, ESV) "For surely it is not angels that he helps, but he helps the offspring of Abraham." (Heb. 2:16, ESV)

(2) **He was to be of the tribe of Judah**. " For it is evident that our Lord was descended from Judah, a tribe with reference to which Moses spoke nothing concerning priests." (Heb. 7:14, NASB)

(3) **He was to be of the house of David**. " In that day the root of Jesse, who shall stand as a signal for the peoples—of him shall the nations inquire, and his resting place shall be glorious." (Isa. 11:10, ESV)

The Prophets described his Character

(1) **His wisdom**. " And the Spirit of Jehovah shall rest upon him, the spirit of wisdom and understanding,

the spirit of counsel and might, the spirit of knowledge and of the fear of Jehovah." (Isa. 11:2, ASV)

(2) **His obedience.** " For I have come down from heaven, not to do my own will but the will of him who sent me." (John 6:38, ESV)

(3) **His love of righteousness.** " You have loved righteousness and hated wickedness; Therefore God, Your God, has anointed You With the oil of joy above Your fellows." (Ps. 45:7, NASB)

(4) **His gentleness and tenderness.** " He will not cry, nor lift up his voice, nor cause it to be heard in the street. A bruised reed will he not break, and a dimly burning wick will he not quench: he will bring forth justice in truth." (Isa. 42:2-3, ASV)

(5) **His compassion.** " The Spirit of the Lord Jehovah is upon me; because Jehovah hath anointed me to preach good tidings unto the meek; he hath sent me to bind up the broken-hearted, to proclaim liberty to the captives, and the opening of the prison to them that are bound." (Isa. 61:1, ASV).

His Betrayal and Trial

As we approach the closing scenes of Christ's life the prophecies become more minute and remarkable.

(1) **The betrayal.** "And I said unto them, If ye think good, give me my hire; and if not, forbear. So they weighed for my hire thirty pieces of silver. And Jehovah said unto me, Cast it unto the potter, the goodly price that I was prized at by them. And I took the thirty pieces of silver, and cast them unto the potter, in the house of Jehovah." (Zech. 11:12-13, ASV)

(2) **His demeanor when on trial**. "He was oppressed, yet when he was afflicted he opened not his mouth; as a lamb that is led to the slaughter, and as a sheep that before its shearers is dumb, so he opened not His mouth." (Isa. 53:7, ASV)

(3) **When crucified, the soldiers were to part his garments among them and cast lots for his vesture.** "They part my garments among them, And upon my vesture do they cast lots." (Ps. 22:18, ASV)

(4) **He was to be numbered with the transgressors**. "Therefore will I divide him a portion with the great, and he shall divide the spoil with the strong; because he poured out his soul unto death, and was numbered with the transgressors; yet he bare the sin of many, and made intercession for the transgressors." (Isa. 53:12, ASV)

(5) **He was to perish amid cruel mocking**. "But I am a worm, and no man; a reproach of men, and despised of the people. All they that see me laugh me to scorn: they shoot out the lip, they shake the head, saying, Commit thyself unto Jehovah; let him deliver him: let him rescue him, seeing he delighted in him." (Ps. 22:6-8, ASV)

His Resurrection and Coronation

(1) **He was to rise from the dead**. "For thou wilt not leave my soul to Sheol; neither wilt thou suffer thy holy one to see corruption." (Ps. 16:10, ASV)

(2) **His ascension was also a subject of prophecy**. "Thou hast ascended on high, thou hast led away captives; thou hast received gifts among men, yea,

among the rebellious also, that Jehovah God might dwell with them." (Ps. 68:18, ASV)

(3) **His coronation is foretold and described**. "I saw in the night-visions, and, behold, there came with the clouds of heaven one like unto a son of man, and he came even to the ancient of days, and they brought him near before him. And there was given him dominion, and glory, and a kingdom, that all the peoples, nations, and languages should serve him: his dominion is an everlasting dominion, which shall not pass away, and his kingdom that which shall not be destroyed." (Dan. 7:13-14, ASV)

The above are only a few of the many predictions made by the Holy Spirit as to the character, life, sacrifice and dominion of our Lord. We notice now the work of the Spirit in, upon and through him.

He Was Conceived By Holy Spirit

"Now the birth of Jesus Christ took place in this way. When his mother Mary had been betrothed to Joseph, before they came together she was found to be with child from the Holy Spirit." (Matt. 1:18, ESV) "The angel answered and said to her, "The Holy Spirit will come upon you, and the power of the Most High will overshadow you; and for that reason the holy Child shall be called the Son of God." – Luke 1:35, NASB

He was Anointed By Holy Spirit

"And when Jesus was baptized, immediately he went up from the water, and behold,the heavens were opened to him, and he saw the Spirit of God descending like a dove and coming to rest on him; and behold,a voice from heaven said, "This is my beloved Son, with whom I am well pleased." (Matt. 3:16-17, ESV) "In those days Jesus came from Nazareth of Galilee and was baptized by John in the Jordan. And when he came up out of the water, immediately he saw the heavens being torn open and the Spirit descending on him like a dove. And a voice came from heaven, 'You are my beloved Son; with you I am well pleased.'" (Mark 1:9-11, ESV) "Now when all the people were baptized, and when Jesus also had been baptized and was praying, the heavens were opened, and the Holy Spirit descended on him in bodily form, like a dove; and a voice came from heaven, "You are my beloved Son; with you I am well pleased."" (Luke 3:21-22, ESV) "And John bore witness: "I saw the Spirit descend from heaven like a dove, and it remained on him. I myself did not know him, but he who sent me to baptize with water said to me, 'He on whom you see the Spirit descend and remain, this is he who baptizes with the Holy Spirit.'" – John 1:32-33

He Was Led By the Holy Spirit

"Then Jesus was led up by the Spirit into the wilderness to be tempted by the devil." (Matt. 4:1) "The Spirit immediately drove him out into the wilderness." (Mark 1:12) "And Jesus, full of the Holy Spirit, returned from the Jordan and was led by the Spirit in the wilderness." – Luke 4:1

He Performed Miracles By the Holy Spirit

"But if I by the Spirit of God cast out demons, then is the kingdom of God come upon you." (Matt. 12:28) "But if I by the finger of God cast out demons, then is the kingdom of God come upon you." – Luke 11:20

He Offered Himself Up Through Holy Spirit

Hebrews 9:14 English Standard Version (ESV)

14 how much more will the blood of Christ, who through the eternal Spirit offered himself without blemish to God, purify our conscience from dead works to serve the living God.

He Was Raised By the Holy Spirit

"If the Spirit of him who raised Jesus from the dead dwells in you, he who raised Christ Jesus from the dead will also give life to your mortal bodies through his Spirit who dwells in you." (Rom. 8:11) "and was declared to be the Son of God in power according to the Spirit of holiness by his resurrection from the dead, Jesus Christ our Lord." (Rom. 1:4)

He Gave the Commission By the Holy Spirit

Acts 1:1-2 English Standard Version (ESV)

The Promise of the Holy Spirit

1 In the first book, O Theophilus, I have dealt with all that Jesus began to do and teach, ² until the day when he was taken up, after he had given commands through the Holy Spirit to the apostles whom he had chosen.

He Ascended and Coronation Was Announced By the Holy Spirit

"Being therefore exalted at the right hand of God, and having received from the Father the promise of the Holy Spirit, he has poured out this that you yourselves are seeing and hearing." (Acts 2:33, ESV) "Let all the house of Israel therefore know for certain that God has made him both Lord and Christ, this Jesus whom you crucified." – Acts 2:36

Thus, the Spirit predicted the coming of Jesus and the great facts of his birth, baptism, anointing, miracles, death, burial and resurrection, ascension and coronation, and then came from the Father to carry on the work of extending his kingdom. In the light of this testimony we can truly say with Paul in 2 Corinthians 12:3: "And I know that this man was caught up into paradise, whether in the body or out of the body I do not know, God knows."

"I have manifested your name to the people whom you gave me out of the world. Yours they were, and you gave them to me, and they have kept your word. Now they know that everything that you have given me is from you. For I have given them the words that you gave me, and they have received them and have come to know in truth that I came from you; and they have believed that you sent me ... While I was with them, I kept them in your name, which you have given me. I have guarded them, and not one of them has been lost except the son of destruction, that the Scripture might be fulfilled ... I have given them your word, and the world has hated them because they are not of the world, just as I am not of the world. 15 I do not ask that you take them out of the world, but that you keep them from the evil one." — John 17:6-8, 12, 14-15, ESV

CHAPTER 6 The Spirit and the Apostles

By Z. T. Sweeney

Updated By Edward D. Andrews

In interpreting Scripture, attention should be paid not only to the speaker and his message but also to the parties addressed. Some passages are universal in their application, others that are national, and still others that are addressed to individuals only. Many promises are addressed to children of God only and do not apply to those who are not citizens of Christ's kingdom. Again, some commands are addressed solely to men in a state of condemnation and have no relevance when applied to the children of God. Christ uttered many things to his chosen ambassadors, chosen to establish his kingdom [over the] earth, which were never intended to be applied to any others. It is a mistake for the Christian of today to make universal, promises that were intended by our Lord for select individuals. It confuses the whole scheme of redemption and makes a mystery out of Scriptures that are entirely clear when proper limitations are made. Things addressed to a chosen few have been wrongly applied to all, and great confusion has resulted from there. It is my purpose in this chapter to notice some of these.

The fourteenth, fifteenth and sixteenth chapters of John contain a record of a private talk with our Lord to the Twelve, and to them alone. Jesus was approaching the close of his earthly ministry. He had chosen his apostles, and they had left all to follow him. He had eaten, slept and spent time with them. He had taught them the great truths upon which his kingdom would be founded. They had learned to depend on him for advice, instruction, comfort and guidance. They confessed this when they said, "Thou hast the words of eternal life."

He was soon to leave them, and knew that they would feel that they were "as sheep without a shepherd." He wishes them to know that they should not be left orphaned. He tells them, "I will pray the Father, and he shall give you another Comforter that he may abide with you forever," or to the remotest age. That is, as long as you shall have need of him. The Greek word translated "forever" does not necessarily mean unlimited duration. It is often applied to much shorter periods, even to a lifetime. Gerald L. Borchert offers us insight into the "Helper" of John 14:16, 26; 15:26; 16:7.

> The term Paraclete (*paraklētos*), rendered "comforter" in the KJV, "counselor" in the RSV, NIV, HCSB, and NLT, "helper" in the TEV and NKJV, and "advocate" in the NRSV, is a verbal adjective carrying a passive force.[47] It is derived from *parakalein* and has the same meaning as *ho parakeklēmenos*, the articular perfect participle that means "the one called alongside." It was sometimes used within the Greek legal system, but in the Roman legal system the comparable Latin word *advocatus* became a technical term referring to a defense counsel.[48]

The term is only used by John in the New Testament and is similarly applied to Jesus in 1 John 2:1, where Jesus is said to be the

---

[47] See Westcott, *John*, 2.189.

[48] Cf. *BAGD*, 618; *TDNT*, 5.800–801.

Christian's Paraclete with the Father. Also by implication John may consider Jesus to be a Paraclete here at John 14:16 because the Spirit of truth is said to be "another" Paraclete. The only other uses of the term in the New Testament are in this Gospel and refer to the Holy Spirit (14:26; 15:26; 16:7).[149] The term does not appear in the Septuagint.[49]

This Paraclete is a distinct gift to the twelve, to take the place of the personal presence and guidance of the leader who is preparing to leave them.

What is the nature of this promised one? By examining the lexicons, we find that Paraclete (Helper) is:

1. One called or sent to assist another.
2. One who pleads the cause of another.
3. A monitor.
4. An instructor.
5. A guide.
6. A helper.
7. A supporter.
8. A comforter.

Of this Paraclete (Helper) Jesus says:

1. Whom the world cannot receive.

---

[149] Cf. Morris, *John*, 587–89.

[49] Gerald L. Borchert, *John 12–21*, vol. 25B, The New American Commentary (Nashville: Broadman & Holman Publishers, 2002), 122–123.

2. He dwelled with you and shall be in you.

3. He shall teach you all things.

4. He shall bring all things to your remembrance whatsoever I have spoken unto you.

5. He shall testify of me.

6. He shall convict the world of sin.

7. He shall convict the world of righteousness.

8. He shall convict the world of judgment.

9. He shall guide you into all truth.

10. He shall show you things to come.

11. He shall receive of mine and show it unto you.

Here we have eleven distinct things that the Paraclete is to do for the apostles.

The apostles in their work of proclaiming Christianity and establishing the church needed all these offices of the Paraclete. They were ignorant and unlearned,[50] humanly speaking, and could never have gone forth to success without this supernatural Paraclete. They took no thought what they should say, for it was given them at the proper time. Others have to take thought. Paul tells Timothy to "Be diligent to present yourself approved to God as a workman who does not need to be ashamed, accurately handling the word of truth." (2 Tim. 2:15, NASB) Timothy had to study because he did not possess the Paraclete. Yet Timothy did possess the gift of the Spirit. "For which cause I put thee

---

[50] Unlearned in the sense of not having been taught by the Jewish teachers at the Jewish schools, like the apostle Paul with Gamaliel. This did not mean that they were unable to read or to write.

in remembrance that thou stir up the gift of God, which is in thee through the laying on of my hands." – 2 Timothy 1:6

Men today are required to study that they may know what to say. A failure to observe this exhortation of the apostle is the reason why a great many do not know what to say. The Paraclete was not only an instructor, but he was an infallible guide. This is evident from the fact that no apostle ever contradicted another nor said anything foolish. I never heard a man of to-day lay claim to being guided "into all truth by the Spirit," who did not say something foolish in the next five minutes. If any man claims the direct guidance of the Spirit to-day, he cannot consistently deny that same claim to others. However, we have all sorts of men teaching all kinds of doctrines, often contradicting each other. Does the Spirit guide one man to preach up Universalism and another man to preach it down! The same is true of Calvinism, Mormonism or any other ism.

This teaching, places the Spirit in a very unenviable position that of preaching four or five different teachings at the same time, each within a half-mile of the other. Suppose a preacher were to do that! What would the people think of him? It would ruin the reputation of any preacher in Christendom. There is something wrong, and that something is to apply to the world the promise of the Paraclete, which was only given to the apostles.

Paul tells Timothy: "what you have heard from me in the presence of many witnesses entrust to faithful men who will be able to teach others also." (2 Tim. 2:2, ESV) Would that not have been a bold or rude, lack of respect on Paul's part if Timothy had the same divine leading as he? Was it not bold or rude, lack of respect in Jude to say that the faith was "once for all delivered to the holy ones," if there were deliverances being constantly made? What need to preach the gospel to the heathen world if God is directly leading men into the truth? What need for a New Testament if all men possess this Paraclete? How can one man deny the claims of another whom he admits to be divinely guided into all truth?

Some had thought that Christ bestowed the Paraclete upon the apostles when he breathed upon them and said, "Receive the Holy Spirit." At best that was a prophetic and not an actual bestowal, for after that onbreathing we find Peter (Acts I) calling upon the assembly of brothers to take a vote as to who should succeed Judas in the apostolic college. If he had possessed the Paraclete at that time, he would not have been compelled to resort to the judgment of his brethren to determine such a question.

Moreover, Christ indicated when the Paraclete would come, by stating the work that would follow his coming: "And when he comes, he will convict the world concerning sin and righteousness and judgment." How did he do this?

1. His first act at his coming was to baptize the apostles in the Spirit and endow them with the Paraclete. "You will be baptized with the Holy Spirit not many days from now." (Acts 1:5)

2. When the Spirit baptized these apostles with divine guidance he began his work of convicting the world through them.

To Convict the World of Sin

(a) Not of sin in general. It is a mistaken idea that the Spirit is sent to convict a man of the sin of lying, stealing or defrauding his neighbor personally. The above passage teaches nothing of the kind, nor does any other passage in the New Testament teach it. There is not a case in the New Testament where the Holy Spirit ever made an issue with a man to convict him personally of sin. The Spirit convicts all men of sin, but it is the Spirit working through the preaching of Spirit-filled men. "And when he comes, he will convict the world concerning sin and righteousness and judgment: concerning sin, because they do not believe in me." (John 16:8-9, ESV) They called him a blasphemer, they rejected him, they took him with wicked hands and crucified and slew him; and the first thrust of the Spirit on the day of Pentecost was at this sinful act of the world: "Let all the house of Israel therefore know for certain that God has made him both Lord and Christ, this Jesus whom you crucified." – Acts 2:36, ESV

The righteousness of Jesus Christ

(b) "Concerning righteousness, because I go to the Father, and you will see me no longer." (John 16:10, ESV) If this passage teaches that men are individually convicted of sin, it also teaches that they are individually convicted of righteousness, and this would be a most herculean task, even for the Spirit, to perform. It is a contradiction of terms to say that the Spirit convicts a man of sin, then, in the next breath, that he convicts the same man of righteousness. And yet, the Spirit was to convict men "of righteousness;" but whose righteousness? "Concerning righteousness, because I go to the Father, and you will see me no longer." (John 16:10) When Jesus was on earth he claimed to be the Son of God; he claimed to come down from heaven; he claimed to be God manifest in the flesh; but, at the same time, he was a "man of sorrows and acquainted with grief." "There was no beauty that we should desire him." On this account the Jews refused to accept him as the Son of God; they denied his claim to divinity and called him a blasphemer for making himself equal with God; they believed that he was unrighteous in making that claim, and Jesus died because his claims were not accepted by his people; but after his death he was crowned with glory and honor at the right hand of the Majesty on high, and the Spirit came to demonstrate the righteous claims Jesus made while on earth. The Spirit came to convict men of the righteousness of Christ, and not their own righteousness.

A simple illustration will probably throw light upon this thought. Forty years ago, my father lived in a little village in the State of Illinois, midway between St. Louis and Indianapolis. One afternoon two young lads, covered with dust and dirt, came to his house and told him they were sons of an elder of a Christian Church in Indiana; that they had been robbed in St. Louis, and were making their way home on foot; they asked for something to eat. My father doubted their claims; he felt that they were impostors; but my mother, who had boys of her own out in the world, and who always believed the best of everybody, said, "We will feed them and care for them during the night." Their wants were supplied, and they were given lodging for the night, and sent on their way the next morning with a good lunch for the day. Six months afterward, I preached in Monroe County, Indiana, and, stopping with one of the elders of the church, two young lads were introduced to me as his boys. They asked me if my father lived in Illinois. I told them he did. They then recounted their experience at my father's home, and said to me, "We would be glad when you return home if you will tell your father that you stopped at our house and that you know we were what we claimed to be when we sought his aid." When I returned to my father's home, I convicted him of the righteousness of those boys in the claim that they set forth, and which he had hitherto doubted. In a similar manner, the Spirit of God came down to convict the world that had rejected the claims of Jesus, of his righteousness in making those claims.

Put on the Complete Armor of God

(c) Paul warns us, "Put on the full armor of God, so that you will be able to stand firm against the schemes of the devil. For our wrestling[51] is not against flesh and blood, but against the rulers, against the powers, against the world-rulers of this darkness, against the wicked spirit forces in the heavenly places." (Eph. 6:11-12) Do we fully understand this? Think about it, Satan the Devil has an invisible, extremely powerful organization of demonic angels. Jesus Christ himself called Satan "the ruler of this world." (John 12:31; 14:30; 16:11) The apostle said that Satan is "the god of this world." – 2 Corinthians 4:4.

This Paraclete continued with the apostles until the end of their ministry, guiding, leading, and showing them "things to come," bringing all things to their remembrance that Christ had spoken unto them. Under this direct and supernatural control, they preached the gospel to all the nations of the earth and established the church with all its officers, ordinances, privileges and duties. They wrote the epistles to the churches and gave to mankind the New Testament, "the perfect law of liberty." The work of the Paraclete being finished, and his mission ended, no man has been guided, shown and directed personally by him

---

[51] Or struggle

since. God does no unnecessary work, and the work of the Paraclete is not necessary now. His work remains in the teachings and lives of the apostles. There are many things in the above-mentioned chapters that rightfully have a universal application, but the special promises concerning the Paraclete are not included in those things.

Ephesians 4:8, 11-13 Updated American Standard Version (UASV)

⁸ Therefore it says,

"When he ascended on high he led captivity captive, and he gave gifts to men."

¹¹ And he gave some as apostles, and some as prophets, and some as evangelists, and some as shepherds and teachers, ¹² for the equipping of the holy ones or the work of ministry, to the building up of the body of Christ; ¹³ until we all attain to the unity of the faith, and of the accurate knowledge[52] of the Son of God, to a mature man, to the measure of the stature which belongs to the fullness of Christ.

---

[52] *Epignosis* is a strengthened or intensified form of *gnosis* (*epi*, meaning "additional"), meaning, "true," "real," "full," "complete" or "accurate," depending upon the context. Paul and Peter alone use *epignosis*.

CHAPTER 7 The Spirit and the Apostolic Church

By Z. T. Sweeney

Updated By Edward D. Andrews

That the Holy Spirit sustained a relation to the apostolic church that it does not sustain to the church of today is clearly evident to the student of the Word of God. The church of the apostolic age had no New Testament as we have today. Hence, the necessity of a more direct and immediate leading than is necessary today. The apostle Paul states the difference between the two when he says: "For we know in part and we prophesy in part, but when the perfect comes, the partial will pass away." (1 Cor 13:9-10, ESV) This is not a contrast between the imperfections of our day and the perfection of heaven, but between the imperfection of the apostolic church and the perfection of the church of today. That which is perfect has come; a perfect revelation of Christian character, a perfect gospel, a perfect "law of liberty," a perfect New Testament.

The apostolic church was limited to knowing in part and prophesying in part. "To each is given the manifestation of the Spirit for the common good. For to one is given through the Spirit the utterance of wisdom, and to another the utterance of knowledge according to the same Spirit, to another faith by the same Spirit, to another gifts of healing by the one Spirit, to another the working of miracles, to another prophecy, to another the ability to distinguish between spirits, to another various kinds of tongues, to another the interpretation of tongues. All these are empowered by one and the same

Spirit, who apportions to each one individually as he wills. —1 Corinthians 12:7-11, ESV.

Now, here was manifestly a condition in the first churches that does not exist today. Here are various direct and supernatural workings that are manifestations of spiritual power resulting from a direct gift of the Spirit to members of apostolic churches. Now, there was a purpose to be accomplished by this special gift of the Spirit. In the fourth chapter of Ephesians, the apostle tells us the purpose of this gift. "And he gave some as apostles, and some as prophets, and some as evangelists, and some as shepherds and teachers, for the equipping of the holy ones or the work of ministry, to the building up of the body of Christ; until we all attain to the unity of the faith, and of the knowledge of the Son of God, to a mature man, to the measure of the stature which belongs to the fullness of Christ." (Eph. 4:11-13, ESV) This gift of the Spirit accompanied the baptism of the Spirit on the day of Pentecost.

This brings us to a very interesting question. Was the promise of the "gift of the Holy Spirit," referred to by Peter on the day of Pentecost, a universal one to all who obey the gospel? Or was it limited to those of the apostolic church who received it that they might manifest it in a supernatural way "to profit along with the rest," or to the profit of all?

There are some who claim that "the gift of the Spirit" is one that belongs to all who obey the gospel to- day. In addition, that it is independent of the instrumentality of the gospel, and is the peculiar heritage of those who repent and are baptized for the remission of sins; that it performs a work in them other than is performed by the Spirit operating through the truth. There are others who claim that the "gift of the Spirit" was a supernatural power and was conferred on persons to qualify them to do the work or works peculiar to the age of miracles that were obtained in the apostolic church. The only way to settle this is by appealing to (1) the consciousness of individuals, (2) to the Word of God.

Before appealing to either of these tribunals, there are a few facts that we must consider. (1) This is the only passage in the New Testament that connects "the gift of the Spirit" with obedience to the gospel in the preaching of the apostles. (Acts 2:37-40) We have remission of sins so connected on various occasions (see Acts 5:31; 10:43; 13:38; 26:18, etc., etc.), but nowhere else is this "gift of the Spirit" promised. If it is to be as universal as "remission of sins," ought it not to have the same prominence in apostolic preaching? This is a major factor in settling the matter. (2) In the only instance in which it is promised it is inexorably connected with baptism for the remission of sins. It is promised to no others, and all others are ruled out by the explicit terms of the promise.

With these facts before us, let us now appeal to the consciousness of the individual. If we consider numbers, it is safe to say that many of those who today claim "the gift of the Spirit" have never been baptized for the remission of sins. They have never performed the conditions upon which the gift was bestowed. Are they competent to testify? Of the remaining few, there is not one who can give any definite reason why he is conscious of the personal indwelling of the Spirit within him. To demonstrate my statement, I appeal to the consciousness of my readers. Are you aware of any influence within you except a holy joy that comes from obedience to the will of God? If you are not, what evidence have you that the Spirit personally dwells in you? So much for the argument from consciousness.

In the paragraph below, this author would argue that it is highly likely that Sweeney is mistaken. This does not take away from the point he is making in this entire chapter. After his paragraph, this author will do a small excursion on what he has said and offer some insight, as well as perspective. – Edward D Andrews.

Now let us appeal to the inspired Word of God. When the apostle Peter promised "the gift of the Spirit," he followed it with the words, "For the promise is for you and for your children and for all who are far off, everyone whom the Lord our God calls to himself." (Ac 2:39, EV) He distinctly states that the gift of the Spirit is in fulfillment of "the promise." Now, is there in the Scripture any promise of a personal indwelling of the Holy Spirit as a result of obedience? Let us search the words of the Master. In **Luke 11:13** our Lord says, "If you then, who are evil, know how to give good gifts to your children, how much more will **the heavenly Father give <u>the Holy Spirit</u> to those who ask him**!" (ESV) This passage may be disposed of by saying that in the original it is a holy spirit and does not refer to the Holy Spirit at all. It represents God's willingness to give **a holy disposition**.

Excursion "Holy Spirit" and Luke 11:13

In the New Testament, we have the phrase "holy spirit" (Gr., *pneuma hagion*) **eighty-seven times**. Without belaboring the subject, we must consider the fact that those who lived in the New Testament era were more used to speaking of "spirits" than we are today. Do not get me wrong, the general population does speak of "spiritual" things to a degree. Many readers likely have heard or used such expressions as "being spirited" or "the human spirit." Of those eighty-seven times, the phrase "holy spirit" is used **forty-two times** with the definite article,[53] which is rendered "the Holy Spirit" and **forty-five times** without the definite article (anarthrous),[54] which can be rendered a number of ways. One might automatically assume that if there is no definite article ("the") in the forty-five times, it should be translated "a holy spirit." This is not really the case because there are Greek grammar rules, which would make the phrase "holy spirit still definite." For example, if there is no definite article with a noun that follows a preposition, it can still be definite. (Smyth 1916, Section 1128) The anarthrous phrase "holy spirit" occurs within a prepositional phrase **twenty-one times**.[55] Thus, Smyth's Greek Grammar rule means that we cannot see these uses of "holy spirit" as being indefinite, but rather a definite, i.e., the Holy Spirit. Another grammatical construction that may cause the definite article to be dropped in Greek is the characteristic of the verb in verbal phrase. The expression "filled with Holy Spirit" is found **fourteen times** in the New Testament without the definite article,[56] which does not mean it is to be taken as

---

[53] For example, Matthew 12:32; Mark 3:29; 12:36; Luke 2:6; 3:22; 10:21; John 14:26; and Acts 1:16 to mention just a few.

[54] First, anarthrous means without the article; second, it should be noted that in English, we have both a definite article "the" and an indefinite article "a" and "an." In biblical Greek, known as Koine (i.e., common) Greek there is only a definite article. Thus, if they want to make something definite, they place their definite article before it. Generally speaking, if the article is missing, whatever is being spoken of is indefinite but this is not always the case. Grammar and syntax can make something definite even without the definite article.

[55] Matthew 1:18, 20; 3:11; Mark 1:8; Luke 3:16; John 1:33; Acts 1:2, 5; 11:16; 13:4; 16:6; Romans 5:5; 9:1; 14:17; 15:16; 1 Corinthians 12:3; 2 Corinthians 6:6; 1 Thessalonians 1:5; 2 Timothy 1:14; Jude 1:20; and 2 Peter 1:21.

[56] Luke 1:5, 35, 41, 67; 4:1; Acts 2:4; 4:8, 34; :65; 7:55; 9:17; 11:24; 13:9; and 13:52.

indefinite. The verb "fill" has objects in the genitive form, which does not need the definite article to establish definiteness, like other forms, i.e., nominative and accusative.

Therefore, we have eighty-five occurrences of the phrase "holy spirit," with forty-five of which that does not have the definite article. However, there are **thirty-two occurrences** where the grammatical or syntactical construction allows the anarthrous phrase "holy spirit" to be definite. Of the thirteen occurrences of the phrase "holy spirit" without the definite article, we can remove another **six times** because the phrase is in the genitive for dative form, which does not need an article in order to be definite. They are Romans 15:13; 1 Thessalonians 1:6; Titus 3:5; Hebrews 2:4; 6:4; and 1 Peter 1:12. Almost all translations render these as definite, namely, "the Holy Spirit. (ASV, ESV, RSV, NASB, HCSB, LEB, and so on)

This leaves **seven occurrences** of the phrase "holy spirit" without the definite article, where no grammar or syntax can be used to see them as definite. Our **Luke 11:13** in the above is one of them.[57] It reads, "If you, although you are evil, know how to give good gifts to your children, how much more will the Father from heaven give (*pneuma* [spirit] *hagion* [holy])[58] to those who ask him?" There is no definite article and "holy" is not in a genitive or dative form, nor is there any

---

[57] The other six occurrences are Acts 8:15, 17-19; Acts 10:38; 19:2; Luke 2:25; and John 20:22.

[58] In Greek, the order of words is not important because the endings at the end of a word will tell the reader whether it is a verb, a noun, and adjective and so on. Moreover, these endings will let the reader know if it is plural, singular, or neuter; whether the verb is indicative, subjunctive, or a participle, present, future, aorist, first, second, or third person, among many other details.

grammar and syntax rules that would allow "holy spirit" to be taken definitely. If Luke specifically meant "the Holy Spirit," he would have had to use the definite article in this phrase. Does this mean that he was not talking about the Holy Spirit here in Luke 11:13 but rather "a holy disposition" as Sweeney argues? This author believes that Sweeney is mistaken but that his attention to this verse is correct. I believe it is a reference to the Holy Spirit. If we sincerely ask God for Holy Spirit, if it is according to his will and purposes, he will not withhold this gift. The question, then, is, in what sense do we receive this gift of "holy spirit" as a guide? Is it like the apostles who were inspired, moved along by Holy Spirit in their penning the Word of God, or by our taking in the inspired by Holy Spirit, inerrant Word of God? I believe it is the latter, which means it is still in harmony with everything said in this book.

End of Excursion

Matthew explains it in the words "If you then, who are evil, know how to give good gifts to your children, how much more will your Father who is in heaven **give good things to those who ask him**!" (Matt. 7:11, ESV) In John 7:38-39 we have recorded another promise: "'Whoever believes in me, as the Scripture has said, 'Out of his heart will flow rivers of living water.' Now this he said about the Spirit, whom those who believed in him were to receive, for as yet the Spirit had not been given, because Jesus was not yet glorified." This is evidently a supernatural gift, as he represents the recipient of it as a fountain from which flows rivers of living water. This is obviously not true of us to-day. Our Savior also dates the bestowal as following his glorification, or on the day of Pentecost. In Mark 16:16-18: "Whoever believes and is baptized will be saved, but whoever does not believe will be condemned. 17 And these signs will accompany those who believe: in my name they will cast out demons; they will speak in new tongues; 18 they will pick up serpents with their hands; and if they drink any deadly poison, it will not hurt them; they will lay their hands on the sick, and they will recover." These five things that accompanied the believers are all supernatural. Of the three promises of Jesus, which are all that are recorded in the New Testament, only two refer to the Holy Spirit, and both of these to its supernatural manifestation. This author says that it does not matter the argument Sweeney is offering for Mark 16:16-18, as has will be evidence in APPENDIX A and B, Mark 16:9-20 are an interpolation into the Bible, which were added by some unknown writer in the second century, meaning they are not part of the original.

If we go back of the Savior to the Old Testament, we find a distinct promise of the gift of the Spirit: "And it shall come to pass afterward, that I will pour out my Spirit upon all flesh; and your sons and your daughters shall prophesy, your old men shall dream dreams, your young men shall see visions: and also upon the servants and upon the handmaids in those days will I pour out my Spirit." (Joel 2:28, 29) This promise is the one quoted by Peter to explain the manifestations on the day of Pentecost to the people drawn together by that wonderful event. From it, he delivers by the Spirit a sermon on the claims of our Lord. He shows that they had taken the Lord by wicked hands and had crucified and slain him; that God had raised him from the dead and had exalted him to his right hand; had given him the promise of the Holy Spirit; that what they saw and heard was the fulfillment of Joel's promise. This promise was not simply to the apostles, for we read in the preceding chapter that the apostles, and the women and Mary the mother of Jesus, and his brethren to the number of one hundred and twenty all continued with one accord in prayer and supplication. "And suddenly there came from heaven a sound like a mighty rushing wind, and it filled the entire house where they were sitting. And divided tongues as of fire appeared to them and rested on each one of them. And they were all filled with the Holy Spirit and began to speak in other tongues as the Spirit gave them utterance." (Acts 2:2-4, ESV) This shows that the gift of the Spirit came upon all the followers Jesus left behind him.

When the apostle's discourse convicted the multitude, they "Now when they heard this they were cut to the heart, and said to Peter and the rest of the apostles, 'Brothers, what shall we do?' And Peter said to them, 'Repent and be baptized every one of you in the name of Jesus Christ for the forgiveness of your sins, and you will receive the gift of the Holy Spirit. For the promise is for you and for your children and for all who are far off, everyone whom the Lord our God calls to himself.'" What promise! Evidently, the promise of God, "I will pour out of my spirit upon all flesh." (Joel 2:28) There is no other promise in the mind of Peter and his hearers, and I know of no other promise the reader can have in mind. This position is amply supported by after-developments. "While Peter was still saying these things, the Holy Spirit fell on all who heard the word. And the believers from among the circumcised who had come with Peter were amazed because the gift of the Holy Spirit was poured out even on the Gentiles. For they were hearing them speaking in tongues and extolling God. Then Peter declared, "Can anyone withhold water for baptizing these people, who have received the Holy Spirit just as we have?'" (Acts 10:44-47). This was in fulfillment of the promise to not only the Jews but also the Gentiles, whom the Jews regarded as "far off."

Paul, speaking to Gentiles, says, "But now in Christ Jesus you who once were far off have been brought near by the blood of Christ." (Eph. 2:13) In this incident "the gift of the Holy Spirit" and "receiving the Spirit" are the same. And when Peter was taken to task for baptizing the Gentiles, he defends himself on the ground that God, who knows the heart, bore witness to them, giving them the Holy Spirit, "the like gift as he did also unto us." In the above instances, Pentecost and the house of Cornelius, the gift of the Spirit was the result of the baptism of the Spirit, the baptism of the Spirit was an outpouring or falling of the Spirit upon the Jews at Pentecost and the Gentiles at the house of Cornelius, to signify his acceptance of both Jew and Gentile into the kingdom of Christ. Paul undoubtedly refers to this when he says, "For by one Spirit we were all baptized into one body, **whether Jews or Greeks**, whether slaves or free, and we were all made to drink of one Spirit." (1 Cor. 12:13, NASB) The baptism of the Spirit ceased when its object, the making of one body out of Jews and Gentiles, was accomplished, but "the gift of the Spirit" did not cease. It was conferred by the laying on of the hands of the apostles through all their lives. A few illustrations may be mentioned from the Scriptures.

The Samaritans. When a bloody persecution arose at Jerusalem, following the death of Stephen, the disciples were scattered and went everywhere preaching the Word. Philip went to the city of Samaria and preached Christ to them. "But when they believed Philip as he preached good news about the kingdom of God and the name of Jesus Christ, they were baptized, both men and women." (Acts 8:12, ESV) "for he had not yet fallen on any of them, but they had only been baptized in the name of the Lord Jesus." (Acts 8:16, ESV) If the gift of the Spirit is to all baptized believers, why did not the

Samaritans receive it? Philip was not an apostle and did not have the power to confer "the gift of the Spirit" by the imposition of hands, and, in order that they might receive this "gift," it was necessary that two apostles, Peter and John, should go to Samaria and lay hands on them, that they might receive the Spirit. Here is a clear case of baptized believers receiving the Holy Spirit by the imposition of hands.

Disciples at Ephesus. In Acts 19 Paul met certain disciples that had received the baptism of John. He showed them that John did not preach a full gospel, which embraced a belief in Christ. "On hearing this, they were baptized in the name of the Lord Jesus. And when Paul had laid his hands on them, the Holy Spirit came on them, and they began speaking in tongues and prophesying." (19:5-6, ESV) This is another clear case of the Spirit being given by the imposition of hands.

Timothy. In 2 Timothy 1:6 Paul tells Timothy: "For this reason I remind you to fan into flame the gift of God, which is in you through the laying on of my hands." This is a third instance of the gift of the Spirit by the imposition of hands, and they form just three more instances than can be found of the Spirit taking his personal "abode in men because they have believed and been baptized."

That the Spirit was imparted to many Christians in a similar way is clear. Paul tells the brothers at Rome, "For I long to see you, that I may impart to you some spiritual gift to strengthen you." (Rom. 1:11, ESV) It was not necessary that he see these brethren to the end that he might proclaim the gospel unto them; but it was necessary that he see them that he might lay hands on them and impart the gift of the Spirit.

We are now enabled to reach two conclusions of importance: First, the "gift of the Spirit" was a supernatural gift for the purpose of enabling the "believers" in apostolic days to work the "signs" which Christ said should accompany them that believe, and ceased when the signs ceased. Second, many of the exhortations of the New Testament writers were to a church whose members were filled with the supernatural power of the Spirit, and should be interpreted in the light of that fact. We give a few examples that fall under this head, "and was declared to be the Son of God in power according to the Spirit of holiness by his resurrection from the dead, Jesus Christ our Lord," (Rom. 1:4). "You, however, are not in the flesh but in the Spirit, if in fact the Spirit of God dwells in you. Anyone who does not have the Spirit of Christ does not belong to him." (Rom. 8:9, ESV) "And not only the creation, but we ourselves, who have the firstfruits of the Spirit, groan inwardly as we wait eagerly for adoption as sons, the redemption of our bodies." (Rom. 8:23, ESV) "I am telling the truth in Christ, I am not lying, my conscience testifies with me in the Holy Spirit." (Rom. 9:1, NASB) "I appeal to you, brothers, by our Lord Jesus Christ and by the love of the Spirit, to strive together with me in your prayers to God on my behalf." (Rom. 15:30, ESV) "e who has prepared us for this very thing is God, who has given us the Spirit as a guarantee." (2 Cor. 5:5, ESV) "Ye were sealed with the Holy Spirit of promise, which is an earnest of our inheritance" (Eph. 1:13, 14). "For through him we both have access in one Spirit to the Father." (Eph. 2:18, ESV) "And do not get drunk with wine, for that is debauchery, but **be filled with the Spirit**." (Eph. 5:18, ESV) "So **if there is any** encouragement in Christ, any comfort from love, any **participation in the Spirit**, any affection and sympathy." (Phil. 2:1, ESV) "Therefore whoever disregards this, disregards not man but God, who gives his Holy Spirit to you." (1 Thess. 4:8, ESV) "For God gave us a spirit not of fear but of power and love and self-control." (2 Tim. 1:7, ESV) "He saved us, not because of works done by us in righteousness, but according to his own mercy, by the washing of regeneration and renewal of the Holy Spirit." (Tit. 3:5, ESV) "While God also bore witness by signs and wonders and various miracles and by gifts of the Holy Spirit distributed according to his will." (Heb. 2:4, ESV) "Or do you suppose it is to no purpose that the Scripture says, 'He yearns jealously over the spirit that he has made to dwell in us'?" (Jas. 4:5, ESV) "But you have been anointed by the Holy One, and you all have knowledge." (1 John 2:20, ESV). "And as for you, **the anointing which you received from him remains in you**, and you do not have need that anyone teach you. But as his anointing teaches you about all things, and is true and is not a lie, and just as it has taught you, you reside in him." (1 John 2:27, LEB). "By this we know that we abide in him and he in us, because he has given us of his Spirit." – 1 John 4:13, ESV

All the above Scriptures become clear if we understand them to apply to a people through whom God was manifesting his presence by supernatural demonstrations, but many of them lack meaning when applied to people of God who no longer exhibit these supernatural powers.

CHAPTER 8 The Spirit and the World

By Z. T. Sweeney

Updated By Edward D. Andrews

Hitherto we have been treating the Holy Spirit in terms of the past, but now we come to the present tense. Is the Holy Spirit a power in the present age? If so, what kind of a power? Is he making an issue with men as a direct power and working upon them immediately, or is he working through an instrumentality, and, if so, what is the instrumentality?

The Spirit is undoubtedly dealing with two classes of persons in his work to-day.

First, those who are not believers, and therefore unconverted and "aliens from the commonwealth of Israel."

Second, those who have believed and obeyed the gospel, and are therefore children of God. We shall devote this chapter to the influence of the Spirit upon the unbelieving world.

In the very nature of things, the work of the Spirit is to make believers out of unbelievers, and convert the perverted. We all believe this. We believe that all believers are made by the power of the Spirit. We differ about whether he exercises that power directly from himself to the individual soul, or whether he exercises that power through the gospel, through the apostles and through Christ's word of truth. Reason, philosophy and experience exhausted themselves in discovering but two methods by which one spirit can exercise an influence over another.

First, a direct mechanical, immediate influence taking possession of the will and influencing the mind of and controlling the speech and actions of the subject. This takes place in hypnotism and is supposed to take place in clairvoyance and clairaudience.

Second, a rational moral influence exerted by ideas impressed upon the mind by teaching and words that represent ideas.

There is, there can be, no third way by which one spirit can influence another. You may study till you are gray-headed or bald-headed, for that matter, and you will discover no other way.

The Holy Spirit has used both of these methods in the past.

1. In the case of the apostles and prophets, he immediately, mechanically and directly controlled their actions and speech, so much so that Jesus told them that under the influence of the Spirit they should take no thought what they should say. "For it is not ye that speak, but the Holy Spirit" (Mark 13:11). "And they were all filled with the Holy Spirit, and began to speak with other tongues, as the Spirit gave them utterance." — Acts 2:4

2. In the case of the men to whom the apostles preached on the day of Pentecost, the Spirit used a rational moral influence through the words of Peter's sermon, which conveyed ideas that swayed their minds and hearts. It is claimed by some that both of these methods are used by the Spirit to-day. The modern teaching concerning the first of these influences is well set forth in the following selection from a widely known book by L.B. Dunn, entitled "The Mission of the Spirit": "Even where the light of the gospel does not shine, and the institutions of the gospel are not enjoyed, there the

Spirit acts directly upon man's heart and conscience, writes the law of God upon his mind, gives him the sense of sin and the need of forgiveness. Hence, wherever man is, there the Comforter is at work upon his heart and mind. The divine influence is imparted unconditionally and irresistibly. The Holy Spirit is ever employed to bring man back to God; and whether he desires it or not, whether he is willing or unwilling, still the Comforter comes to him with his heavenly illumination, his divine influence, convincing him of sin, and his consequent need of the mercy of God. May I not truly say that man really has no choice in the matter as to whether he will or will not have this divine influence upon his soul? He is, he must be, enlightened and convinced, whether he will hear or forbear, whether he will be saved or damned. He cannot prevent the entrance of the Spirit into his heart."

In connection with the above, we quote also from a sermon in "The Baptist Pulpit," by Rev. J.W. Hayhurst: "God has given us no means by which the conversion of sinners, or the general revival of religion, can be effected, irrespective of the direct agency of the Spirit. The gospel itself will not do it."

These quotations give us a pretty clear and explicit statement of the theory of the direct mechanical and immediate operation of the Holy Spirit upon the human spirit.

The second method is aptly stated by an editorial which appeared in the Sunday School Times during the year 1908: "It is a strange fact that, notwithstanding the explicitness and uniformity of the New Testament teachings on this subject, there is a widespread popular opinion that the Holy Spirit's work is directly and immediately on or in the heart of the unbeliever, without the intervention or agency of the Christian whatever. To hear what is said in the sermons, or sung in the hymns, or prayed in the prayers of many Christians, one might believe that the Holy Spirit is sent directly to the unbelieving sinner, to strive with him, to show him his sin, and to point him to, the Savior; and that therefore the Christian preacher or teacher has rather to wait the results of this work of the Spirit, than to be the instrument or the avenue of this work. Many a Christian seems to think that the Holy Spirit's work is that of a revival preacher, in moving sinners to repentance by a direct appeal to their consciences and understandings, instead of stirring up Christians to appeal, in the power of the Spirit, to unbelievers to believe and turn to God. It is true that, in this present dispensation of the Spirit, all power in the evangelizing of the world, and in the swaying of the hearts of men toward Christ and in the service of Christ, is primarily with the Holy Spirit. But it is also true that the Holy Spirit, according to the Bible teachings, works in and by and through believers in Jesus. Hence if one who is not a believer in Jesus is to be won to discipleship, the question is not, 'Will the Holy Spirit work on his mind immediately, or will the Holy Spirit work through one who already believes?' for that question the Bible has already answered. The Holy Spirit can use the written words, like the spoken words, of a chosen messenger of God to an unbelieving soul. But in every case the Spirit reaches the believer mediately (indirectly), not immediately."

Now, these theories are directly contradictory. If one is true, the other cannot be. The only question to decide is as to which one is true. Let us examine these theories in the light of reason, revelation and experience. If the Holy Spirit works directly and immediately on the heart of man, surely there should be some tangible evidence of it given in such a striking way as to demonstrate the truth of the theory. But the experience of Christendom for nineteen centuries fails to furnish a single unquestioned evidence of it. The proof of the theory is made to hinge upon far-fetched inferences drawn from Scripture statements, and even these fail to furnish the evidence sought. Let us notice some of the Scriptures that are relied upon to prove a direct operation of the Spirit in the conversion of sinners:

1. "A new heart also will I give you, and a new spirit will I put within you; and I will take away the stony heart out of your flesh, and I will give you a heart of flesh. And I will put my Spirit within you, and cause you to walk in my statutes, and ye shall keep mine ordinances, and do them" (Ezek. 36:26, 27). This passage has been much relied upon to prove the theory of an abstract operation of the Spirit upon the sinner in conversion. Its failure to support the theory is evidenced by the following facts:

(1) The Lord was not talking about the conversion of a sinner, but the renewal of Israel as a people.

(2) The passage says nothing about the work of the Holy Spirit.

(3) There is nothing mentioned in the passage that could not have been accomplished by ordinary means.

(4) The very point to be proven is assumed.

2. "But their minds were hardened. For to this day, when they read the old covenant, that same veil remains unlifted, because only through Christ is it taken away. 15 Yes, to this day whenever Moses is read a veil lies over their hearts. 16 But when one turns to the Lord, the veil is removed." (2 Cor. 3:14-16, ESV) Just what is found here to prove a direct operation of the Spirit would be difficult to say. The apostle is speaking of the Jews

reading the Scriptures with a veil, which blinds them. The veil was undoubtedly a false interpretation, which prevented their seeing Christ in their Scriptures. If they had not this wrong interpretation, they would see Christ and their Scriptures would be plain. As it was, they were dark and mysterious. The apostle tells what will remove the veil: "When they shall turn to the Lord," the veil shall be taken away. There is nothing in the whole passage that even hints at an immediate operation of the Spirit.

3. "For we are his workmanship, created in Christ Jesus for good works, which God prepared beforehand, that we should walk in them." (Eph. 2:10, ESV) There is nothing here to even hint at a direct operation. It says the Ephesians were created in Christ Jesus (not in the Holy Spirit) unto good works. If the reader wishes to learn by what means they were so created, let him turn to chapter 1, verse 13, and he will obtain the information: "In whom ye also, having heard the word of the truth, the gospel of your salvation,—in whom, having also believed, ye were sealed with the Holy Spirit of promise." That is something to the point. They "heard the word of truth," the gospel of their salvation. Then, after they believed, they "were sealed with the Holy Spirit of promise." There is nothing in the passage to warrant the teaching of a special operation to enable them to believe.

4. "One who heard us was a woman named Lydia, from the city of Thyatira, a seller of purple goods, who was a worshiper of God. The Lord opened her heart to pay attention to what was said by Paul." (Acts 16:14, ESV) This is relied upon to prove a direct work of the Spirit upon Lydia that she might hear and believe. The very thing to be proved is again assumed. True, the Lord opened Lydia's heart, but he did not do so that she might "receive the word," for Paul had already preached it to

her. Her heart was opened that "she gave heed to the things spoken by Paul." Before she heard Paul, she had a narrow, bigoted Jewish heart. After she heard the preaching, her heart was opened to attend to the things she had heard. That is, she obeyed the gospel. Nothing about the Holy Spirit in the entire history.

5. "'And I will ask the Father, and he will give you another Helper, to be with you forever, even the Spirit of truth, whom the world cannot receive because it neither sees him nor knows him. You know him, for he dwells with you and will be in you.'" (John 14:16-17, ESV) As I have elsewhere shown, this passage has a private and peculiar application to the apostles, and not to the world of mankind. It specifically states "the world cannot receive" this Comforter. That kills it as a proof-text that the world "must receive it" before it can believe. Those who affirm a direct operation of the Spirit on "the world" make a clear-cut issue with the Savior.

6. "I planted, Apollos watered, but God gave the growth." (1 Cor. 3:6, ESV) Those who use this to prove a special operation of the Spirit make it mean, "I have planted the word and Apollos has watered it, but God by a special work of the Holy Spirit makes the increase of the word." This is a false interpretation, as the apostle was not speaking of "the word" at all. How could Apollos "water the word"? The apostle was speaking of the congregation at Corinth, which he had planted and Apollos had tended, and which, under the care of God, had made increase. There is nothing in the passage about the Holy Spirit.

7. "While Peter was still saying these things, the Holy Spirit fell on all who heard the word." (Acts 10:44). This has reference to God's signifying his acceptance of the Gentiles by an outpouring similar to the one on the

day of Pentecost. It was purely a supernatural act, and has never been repeated since that day. But even then it would not prove the necessity of an operation of the Spirit, that men might hear the gospel and believe it. The record says, "The Holy Spirit fell on all who heard the word." (Acts 10:44, ESV) Cornelius was told by the angel to send for Peter, "'and he will speak words to you by which you will be saved, you and all your household.'" – Acts 11:14, NASB

8. "The natural person does not accept the things of the Spirit of God, for they are folly to him, and he is not able to understand them because they are spiritually discerned. The spiritual person judges all things, but is himself to be judged by no one." (1 Cor. 2:14-15, ESV) This is held to be one of the strongest passages to confirm the teaching of the necessity of a direct operation of the Holy Spirit to enable a man to hear and to believe the gospel. A brief examination of the context will show that such an idea was not in the mind of the apostle at all. The apostle is not even speaking of conversion when he uses the language. He is speaking of inspiration. The spiritual man in Paul's mind was a man inspired by the Spirit, and the natural man was an uninspired man. If the reader will turn to the ninth verse of the chapter and read to the conclusion of the chapter, and place "uninspired" where he finds "natural," and "inspired" where "spiritual" is found, the passage will be as clear as a sunbeam. "The things of the Spirit" are things produced by the Spirit, which needed an inspired man to explain. The day of Pentecost was a "thing of the Spirit," and there was not an uninspired man in all that great throng that could understand it. The best solution they could give was, "These men are drunk," but Peter, an inspired man, explained in inspired language that "this is what was uttered through the prophet Joel: 'And in the last days it

shall be, God declares, that I will pour out my Spirit on all flesh.'" (Acts 2:16-17, ESV) When these natural (uninspired) men heard Peter's (inspired) spiritual explanation, they could understand it. They did understand it and obeyed it to the number of three thousand. Nebuchadnezzar's vision was a "thing of the Spirit," and there was not a natural (uninspired) man in all his realm that could interpret it. But Daniel, a spiritual (inspired) man, explained it in spiritual language and then all could understand it. There is nothing in the passage to support the theory of a direct operation to enable man to understand the gospel.

9. "God exalted him at his right hand as Leader and Savior, to give repentance to Israel and forgiveness of sins." (Acts 5:31, ESV) This passage is used because it speaks of Christ giving repentance. They infer that is done by a direct operation of the Spirit. But the passage says nothing as to how he grants repentance. Christ gives many things that are not the result of a direct operation of the Spirit. The very next verse says God gives "the Holy Spirit to all them that obey him." This directly contradicts the theory of the necessity of a direct operation of the Spirit to enable men to obey him.

10. "No one can come to me unless the Father who sent me draws him. And I will raise him up on the last day." (John 6:44) This is greatly relied upon to show the necessity of an irresistible drawing before men can come to Christ. The word "draw," in the Scriptures, is a translation of two words in the original. One means to draw by force, "to drag;" the other means to "entice, allure or persuade," that men are drawn by moral arguments, or "allured." In the next verse, Christ tells how men are drawn. "Everyone who has heard and learned from the Father comes to me." (John 6:45, ESV) Christ draws men by "teaching," and they come as result of

"learning." That is why he told his disciples to "go teach all nations." That is Christ's method of drawing.

Now, I have selected ten of the strongest passages in the New Testament that support the theory of a direct operation of the Spirit before men are qualified to hear and obey the gospel. If it is not taught in the above passages, it is not taught in the Bible. When rightly considered, not one of them even leans toward the theory. Are we not justified in saying that the theory is not supported by the Scriptures! Now, how are persons made believers? Hear the word of God:

1. "For I am not ashamed of the gospel, for it is the power of God for salvation to everyone who believes, to the Jew first and also to the Greek." (Rom. 1:16, ESV) Now, here is the unequivocal statement that God's power to save is lodged in the gospel. In all ages of Christianity there is not a record of a single soul ever being saved without the presence of this power. But this is not a magical power. It must be heard in order that it produce faith. But how shall they hear without a preacher and how shall he preach except he be sent? The order is, then, (1) send, (2) preach, (3) hear, (4) believe, (5) obey, (6) saved. Now, this is the order of the Savior's commission to his followers. "Go therefore and make disciples of all nations, baptizing them in the name of the Father and of the Son and of the Holy Spirit, teaching them to observe all that I have commanded you. And behold, I am with you always, to the end of the age." (Matt. 28:19-20, ESV) That is our marching order to-day.

2. "The brothers immediately sent Paul and Silas away by night to Berea, and when they arrived, they went into the synagogue of the Jews. Now these were more noble-minded than those in Thessalonica, who

received the word with all readiness of mind,[59] examining the Scriptures daily to see whether these things were so." (Acts 17:11-12) Here were believers made by searching the Scriptures and by receiving the Word with all "readiness of mind." The same method will make believers of unbelievers today.

3. "For if you were to have countless tutors in Christ, yet you would not have many fathers, for in Christ Jesus I became your father through the gospel." (1 Cor. 4:15, NASB) No clearer statement could be made as to the power exercised in begetting men to a new life. They are begotten through the gospel.

4. "In the exercise of His will He brought us forth by the word of truth, so that we would be a kind of first fruits among His creatures." (Jas. 1:18, NASB) This is as clear as the one above it. The Word of truth brings us forth.

5. "'For the heart of this people has become dull, With their ears they scarcely hear, And they have closed their eyes, Otherwise they would see with their eyes, Hear with their ears, And understand with their heart and return, And I would heal them.'" (Matt. 13:15) To be healed, one must be converted; to be converted, one must understand with the heart; to understand with the heart, one must perceive and hear. But the people the Lord mentions were not healed. Why? Because they were not converted. Why were they not converted? Because they had not perceived with their eyes and heard with their ears. Why had they not seen and heard! "Their ears are dull of hearing, And their eyes they have closed; Lest

---

[59] Or with all *eager readiness of mind*. The Greek word *prothumias* means that one is eager, ready, mentally prepared to engage in some activity.

at any time they should see with their eyes, And hear with their ears." Men talk of the Bible being a sealed book. They would better talk of sealed eyes, ears and hearts, as does the Savior.

CHAPTER 9 The Parting Word

By Z. T. Sweeney

Updated By Edward D. Andrews

Blasphemy against the Spirit

This is a subject that is intensely interesting to many people. They imagine that in some way unknown to themselves they may have committed this act, and it causes them great concern. I will say that such people need have no alarm. The man who has actually committed this sin never feels any alarm about it. He is the last man to feel concern over it. By reading the twelfth chapter of Matthew, the reader can obtain a clear view of this sin. Jesus was being hounded by the Pharisees, who had determined to procure his death at all hazards. They were watching, exaggerating and criticizing everything he did.

He went on a Sabbath day through the field of corn and his disciples plucked and ate some of the corn. There was an immediate outcry of "The Sabbath is violated." Again, Jesus healed the man with a withered hand and the Pharisees went out and held a council to plan his destruction. Again, there was brought to him a man possessed of a devil, rendering him blind and dumb. Jesus healed him by casting out the devil, so that he "both saw and heard." The Jews had always regarded casting out devils as a direct work of the Spirit of God. The people are amazed, and proclaimed him the Son of David, or the Messiah. The Pharisees could not deny the fact, but they said: "He does it by Beelzebub, the prince of devils."

These three incidents show a disposition on their part to deliberately reject all testimony contrary to their plan to compass his death. They had rendered their verdict in advance and were not open to conviction, no matter what testimony might be offered. Jesus tells them that if he casts out devils by Beelzebub, then Satan is divided against himself. "'But if it is by the Spirit of God that I cast out demons, then the kingdom of God has come upon you.'" (Matt. 12:28, ESV) "'Therefore I tell you, every sin and blasphemy will be forgiven people, but the blasphemy against the Spirit will not be forgiven. And whoever speaks a word against the Son of Man will be forgiven, but whoever speaks against the Holy Spirit will not be forgiven, either in this age or in the age to come.'" (Matt. 12:31-32) That these men had committed, or were in great danger of committing, this blasphemy is evident from the caution uttered above.

When a man to-day reaches the comprehensive state of mind that he is going to reject Jesus over any and all evidence, he has gone into the house, shut and locked the door and thrown away the key. God cannot reach him. Such a man will be let alone by the Spirit of God. That Paul understood this condition to be unpardonable, we read in Heb. 6:4-6, "For in the case of those who have once been enlightened and have tasted of the heavenly gift and have been made partakers of the Holy Spirit, and have tasted the good word of God and the powers of the age to come, and then have fallen away, it is impossible to renew them again to repentance, since they again crucify to themselves the Son of God and put him to public shame." Paul says it is impossible to renew such a one to repentance. Why? "Seeing they crucify to themselves the Son of God afresh." That is, they have reached the same state of mind the Pharisees had who crucified him the first time. Men can commit that same act to-day, but when they do it they lose all concern regarding the consequences. As long as one has concern, he may rest assured that he has not blasphemed the Holy Spirit.

The Fruit of the Spirit

The Excursion from the *Holman New Testament Commentary* that lies below is true but we should realize that the fruit of the Spirit are character qualities determined by how we act, i.e., general marks and qualities of our life that are revealed in how we act toward others. How do we acquire these general marks and qualities though? Once we accept Christ is there some miraculous indwelling of the Holy Spirit that changes every wordy quality that we former had and immediately gives us an entirely new personality? No, we acquire these qualities or characteristics by putting on the new person over time, by taking the Word of God into our minds and hearts, applying it in our lives.

Excursion

We need to rethink a number of long-standing interpretations of the fruit of the Spirit. Because the word *fruit* is singular, commentators commonly view the nine characteristics listed under the fruit of the spirit as a unit. This would mean that all nine characteristics are always produced completely in every believer. This would be like picking a cluster of fruit from an unusual vine that always has on it a grape, banana, apple, peach, pear, plum, raspberry, blackberry, and blueberry.

Like English, the Greek language does not require the "singular" idea, but has a collective sense. All Christians have areas in which they grow more rapidly and securely than in other areas. If, since becoming a Christian, a person grew rapidly in love, patience, and kindness but still struggled with self-discipline in eating, must we deny that the growth in love, patience, and kindness has anything to do with the Holy Spirit? That goes too far. The text in no way requires us to interpret the fruit that narrowly, nor does such an interpretation line up with reality.

I also doubt interpretations that make the list of nine characteristics a complete list. Instead, I think it was intended to be representative. This becomes clearer when we contrast it, as Paul does, with the acts of the flesh in verses 19–21. Does anyone believe that the fifteen acts in those verses are an exhaustive list? For example, lying is not on the list. Gluttony is missing. Materialism is not found. Murder is omitted. This is not a complete list of sinful acts.

Nor is the ninefold fruit of the Spirit a comprehensive list of character traits for the Christian. Faith and hope—two of the three great theological virtues (faith, hope, and love: 1 Cor. 13) are missing. Are they not fruit of the Spirit? Thankfulness, gratitude, forgiveness, moral purity, and humility are highly held characteristics elsewhere in Scripture but missing here. The list here includes only some of the fruit of the Spirit.

The fruit of the Spirit are not emotions. They are character qualities determined by how we act, not how we feel. For example, we may get angry (an emotion), but if we do not act unkindly in our anger, we may still have manifested the fruit of the Spirit. We may be deeply agitated or fearful about a life circumstance and still manifest the fruit of the Spirit. How? By not rejecting God, lashing out at people, or acting immorally but rather trusting God and doing the right thing in our agitation and fear. We are sometimes led to believe that the fruit of the Spirit equals constant emotional tranquillity. Yet we often have no control over our emotions. If we get angry, we are angry, and if we tell ourselves that we ought not to be angry, it does not always make the anger go away. We can, however, control whether we sin in our anger. That is why the Bible says, "In your anger do not sin" (Eph. 4:26). It does not say the anger is necessarily sin. It does say that we are not to let our anger (an emotion) cause us to sin (an act). As long as we act properly, we are manifesting the fruit of the Spirit.

Contemplating his coming crucifixion when the sin of the world would be placed on him, Jesus was grieved and sorrowing to the point of death in the Garden of Gethsemane. Still he did not sin. He did not forfeit the fruit of the Spirit because his sorrow and grief (emotions) did not destroy his life characteristics of love, joy, and peace. He still loved people, which is why he was willing to go to the cross when he didn't have to. He still had joy: "for the joy set before him endured the cross" (Heb. 12:2). Jesus also had peace because he knew that God was in control, that he was moving all things to a good end, and that in the end all would be well.

The fruit of the Spirit are general marks and qualities of our life that are revealed in how we act toward others, even though, from time to time, emotions might *seem* to crowd them out. They, however, do not or need not.[60]

End of Excursion

Some would argue that the Spirit of God "is not actively involved in the world today." However, this is false. It is not a question of what the Holy Spirit is doing but how the Spirit is doing it. The Holy Spirit's effect on the unbelievers of the world is only as good as the evangelism and witnessing of Christians. The Holy Spirit is reaching the hearts and minds of the unbelievers through the Spirit inspired, inerrant Word of God, the truth that will appeal to the intellect and heart of those who are receptive. The Spirit of God never led any man to contradict the Word, which the Spirit has so clearly revealed. The entire Christian life is a life of faith. It begins, continues and ends in faith. "God is no respecter of persons, but in every nation he that fears God and works righteousness is accepted of him." "The sword of the Spirit" is "the word of God." – Acts 10:35; Ephesians 6:17

---

[60] Max Anders, *Galatians-Colossians*, vol. 8, Holman New Testament Commentary (Nashville, TN: Broadman & Holman Publishers, 1999), 72–73.

APPENDIX A Is Speaking in Tongues a Biblical Teaching?

An extraordinary gift conveyed through the Holy Spirit to a number of disciples starting at Pentecost 33 C.E. that made it possible for them to speak or otherwise glorify God in a tongue in addition to their own.

What Was the Reason for the Speaking in Tongues?

Immediately before his ascension to heaven, Jesus told those who were looking on: "you will receive power when the Holy Spirit has come upon you, and you will be my witnesses in Jerusalem and in all Judea and Samaria, and to the end of the earth." (Acts 1:8, ESV) First, this witnessing campaign was to be of epic proportions; and second, it was to be brought about with the help of the Holy Spirit.

Our modern-day world allows the spread of the gospel to the other side of the globe within a millisecond and in any language. In the first-century, the good news was spread either in written form, orally, or both. Therefore, the ability to be miraculously able to speak a foreign language in the melting pot of that Roman Empire would have been greatly appreciated. This miracle was first realized at the Pentecost 33 C.E. celebration, as the first-century Christians began to witness to the Jews and proselytes in Jerusalem.

Acts 2:5-11, 41 English Standard Version (ESV)

5 Now there were dwelling in Jerusalem Jews, devout men from every nation under heaven. 6 And at

this sound the multitude came together, and they were bewildered, because each one was hearing them speak in his own language. 7 And they were amazed and astonished, saying, "Are not all these who are speaking Galileans? 8 And how is it that we hear, each of us in his own native language? 9 Parthians and Medes and Elamites and residents of Mesopotamia, Judea and Cappadocia, Pontus and Asia, 10 Phrygia and Pamphylia, Egypt and the parts of Libya belonging to Cyrene, and visitors from Rome, 11 both Jews and proselytes, Cretans and Arabians—we hear them telling in our own tongues the mighty works of God." 41 So those who received his word were baptized, and there were added that day about three thousand souls.

A major change was in the offing. The Jews had followed the lead of their religious leaders in the last act of rebellion, resulting in their rejection as his people. The Mosaic Law was being replaced with the law of Christ. This does not mean that no Jew could be received into the newly founded Christian congregation. To the contrary, the next three and half years would be only the Jewish people, who would make up this new way to God. As was the case with Moses, there was to be a sign, miraculous events, which included the speaking in tongues, this as evidence to those, whose heart was receptive to the truth that the Son of God had come, had given his life for them, and ascended back to heaven. Exodus 19:16-19

Speaking in tongues in Acts 2 is evidentiary. The unique speech is demonstrable proof that something supernatural has happened to the 120 disciples of Jesus. Tongues are the sign that these people have received the promise given by Jesus in Acts 1:5, "You will be baptized with the Holy Spirit not many days from now." This sign was clear enough so that all of those present for the Feast of Weeks were able to see that an impossible event was actually happening. The language speech in this chapter has a second, though subordinate, purpose—the communication of the gospel to people of a foreign tongue.[61]

However, there was much labor to be done. Beginning in 36 C.E., with the conversion of Cornelius, an uncircumcised Gentile, the gospel got underway in its spread to non-Jewish people of every nation. (Acts, chap. 10) In truth, so swiftly did it spread that by about 60 C.E., the apostle Paul could say that the gospel had been "proclaimed in all creation that is under heaven." (Col. 1:23) Consequently, by the time of the last apostles death (John c. 100 C.E.), Jesus' faithful followers had made disciples all the way through the Roman Empire—in Asia, Europe, and Africa!

Spread of Christianity in the first century[62]

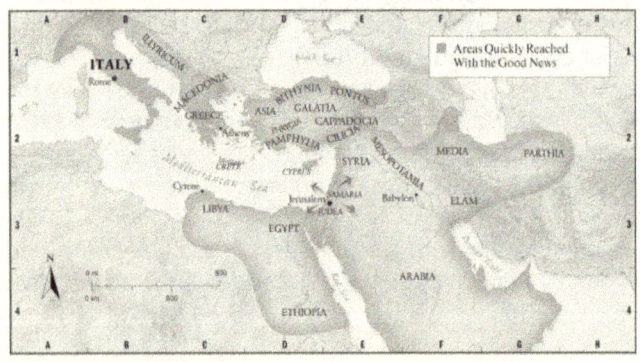

---

[61] Chad Brand, "Tongues, Gift Of", in Holman Illustrated Bible Dictionary, ed. Charles Draper, Archie England, Steve Bond et al., 1605 (Nashville, TN: Holman Bible Publishers, 2003).

[62] (Acts 1:8; 2:1-4, 11; 2:37-41; Ac 5:27, 28, 40-42; 6:7; 8:1, 4, 14-17; 10:1-48; 11:20, 21)

Modern-day Speaking in Tongues

Among those 'speaking in tongues' today are Pentecostals and Baptists, also Roman Catholics, Episcopalians, Methodists, Lutherans, and Presbyterians. Jesus said, "When the Spirit of truth comes, he will guide you into all the truth ..." Would the Pentecostals or the Baptists, who "speak in tongues" suggest that the Roman Catholics, who "speak in tongues" have been 'guided into all the truth,' by the Holy Spirit, as well as the other way around. If modern-day "speaking in tongues" is truly, the same as the first century, and it is evidence proof that a person has Holy Spirit; then, all of the above groups would equally have to be the true path to God.

There is certainly mixed feeling over the revival of speaking in tongues at the beginning of the 20th century. Many see it as nothing more than excessiveness of unhinged persons, doing nothing more than drawing attention to themselves. On the other hand, many see it as the second Pentecost, identical to the occurrence of speaking with tongues in 33 C.E. There is a difference though for the modern-day counterpart where speaking in unknown tongues occurs. A rapturous explosion of jumbled sounds usually initiates it. Many who have been present at such occasions are unable to understand the chaotic speech, as is the case with all others who are present as well as the speaker himself.

Indeed, any reasonable person is moved to ask 'where the benefit in such unknown tongues is, and where the interpreters are?' It is true that there are some, who claim to interpret this incomprehensible speech, yet here again there exist credibility because different explanations are offered for the same speech. In an attempt at removing this difficulty, they offer that God has simply given a different interpretation to these ones. However, they are unable to remove the stain that some of this speech has been base, degrading and depraved. Ronald E. Baxter, in his book *Charismatic Gift of Tongues*, mentions an example where a man refused to interpret the speech of a woman who spoke in the so-called 'gift of tongues,' saying, "The language was the vilest of the vile." This is hardly in harmony with the first-century Christian congregation, where tongues were used for "building up the church." 1 Corinthians 14:4-6, 12, 18.

Still, some have heard the interpretation of what they perceive to be a breathtaking message and believe with their whole heart that God is using this unintelligible speech to give messages to his people. The only problem with this is that Muhammad, Joseph Smith, and others make the same kind of argument. The book of Mormon is the supposed second testament of Christ for millions of Mormons. However, like the modern-day speaking in tongues, we are told very clearly to not go beyond what is written, do not add, nor take away, and that there would be no more miraculous messages until after Armageddon, where more books would be made available. Further still, what could be added by the unintelligible speech that is not available by means of Jesus Christ and the apostles through the Greek New Testament: "All Scripture is breathed out by God and profitable for teaching, for reproof, for correction, and for training in righteousness, that the man of God may be competent, equipped for every good work." 2 Timothy 3:16, 17; Deut. 4:12; Gal 1:8; Rev 20:12; 21:18, 19

As is quite clear from the New Testament itself, the gift of tongues was for a congregation that was in its infancy, and was needed for the preaching of the gospel and the building up the church. However, this is no longer the case: "But even if we or an angel from heaven should preach to you a gospel contrary ["at variance with," *The New English Bible*] to the one we preached to you, let him be accursed."—Galatians 1:8.

Thus then, the gift of tongues is no longer needed, and there is no Biblical foundation for supposing that it is an element of modern-day Christianity. In fact, it is unlikely that it ever survived to the middle of the second-century C.E. At present, the Bible is whole and extensively obtainable, and the Word of God is all that we require. This book alone is a road map to an approved relationship with the Father and the Son, which leads to life eternal. John 17:3; Revelation 22:18, 19

The primary verse to consider reads, "For one who speaks in a tongue speaks not to men but to God; for no one understands him, but he utters mysteries in the Spirit." (1 Cor. 14:2, ESV) When considering this verse, he should keep verses 13-19 of the same chapter in mind.

In other words, those who speak in a tongue speak to God as opposed to men **if** he does not have an interpreter for his speech that is to men who are listening. That is to say, the speaking in tongues is meaningless to the men listening, who do not know (understand) the foreign language as given miraculously through the Holy Spirit. It is for this very reason that Paul says, "no one understands." It could also have been that even the speaker himself of the foreign language did not understand what he was saying because he was not also given the power to interpret (translate). Therefore, without an interpreter, be it himself or another, his speech would only be understood by God, i.e., would be speech only to God, as opposed to men. This is why the apostle Paul would say that if there were no interpreters present, the one speaking in a foreign tongue, should also pray for the gift of interpretation as well. This is so he can also speak to men in a beneficial manner, as well as bring praise to God.

It is Paul, in the first-century, who through the Corinthian congregation sat straight those who had become spellbound and awestruck with the gift of tongues, behaving juvenile, young in the Spirit. While the gift of tongues had its purpose, these ones acted as though it was the most important aspect of the Christian church. (1 Corinthians 14:1-39) The apostle Paul made several things very clear: it was not even a gift that all possessed. Moreover, it did not contribute as an identifying mark of a true Christian, or lead to salvation. Moreover, it was second to the gift of prophecy [proclaiming]. (Elwell, 2001, 1207) Therefore, this gift was not some marker that identified a person as a true Christian, nor was it required to receive the gift of life. 1 Corinthians 12:29, 30; 14:4, 5

What is the Real Force Behind Today's Speaking in Tongues?

There is no doubt that the charismatic church leaders of the 20th century are the impetus behind the resurgence of the speaking in tongues phenomena, pushing their flock members through emotionalism and coercion to achieve this alleged gift. This emotional duress is brought on by these church leaders, who exclude any who are unable to speak in tongues, and treat the other members of the church as superior for their ability to talk in tongues. Therefore, the motivating factor is not the Spirit, not to build up the church, not the glorification of God, but to belong.

Should Christians be identified by their ability to "speak in tongues"?

John 13:35 English Standard Version (ESV)

³⁵ By this all people will know that you are my disciples, if you have love for one another."

1 Corinthians 13:1 English Standard Version (ESV)

If I speak in the tongues of men and of angels, but have not love, I am a noisy gong or a clanging cymbal.

Jesus made the Great Commission all too clear when he said, you will receive power when the Holy Spirit has come upon you, and you will be my witnesses in Jerusalem and in all Judea and Samaria, and to the end of the earth." (Ac 1:8) He had instructed them and us to "Go therefore and make disciples of all nations, teaching them" (Matt 28:19-20). Moreover, he had earlier stressed that this was the last sign before the end of this age, by saying, "this gospel of the kingdom will be proclaimed throughout the whole world as a testimony to all nations, and then the end will come." (Matt 24:14) Do we see this being done by the charismatic groups, who advocate "speaking in tongues"? When was the last time you saw a Pentecostal come to your door, proclaiming the Good News? When was the last time you were out, and a Pentecostal witnessed to you? What Pentecostal church have you ever been to that has an evangelism program, to train its members to evangelize their community?

This gift of tongues is possible by mass hysteria. Worse still, the spirit directing this movement may very well not be the Holy Spirit. "She followed Paul and us, crying out, these men are servants of the Most High God, who proclaim to you the way of salvation.' And this she kept doing for many days. Paul, having become greatly annoyed, turned and said to the spirit, 'I command you in the name of Jesus Christ to come out of her.' And it came out that very hour." (Acts 16:17, 18) The apostle Paul cautioned, "Satan disguises himself as an angel of light." (2 Corinthians 11:14) By seeking a Biblical gift that is no more, these ones have made themselves possible victims of "the lawless one [who] is by the activity of Satan with all power and false signs and wonders, and with all wicked deception for those who are perishing, because they refused to love the truth and so be saved." (2 Thessalonians 2:9, 10) However, some might ask:

Does not Mark 16:17, 18 (NKJ) show that the gi ft of 'speaking with new tongues' would be a sign, so as to recognize believers?

Mark 16:17-18 New King James Version (NKJV)

[17] And these signs will follow those who believe: In My name they will cast out demons; **they will speak with new tongues**; [18] they will take up serpents; and if they drink anything deadly, it will by no means hurt them; they will lay hands on the sick, and they will recover."

First, there is the telling fact that two of the oldest and most highly respected Bible manuscripts, the Vaticanus 03 and the Sinaiticus 01, do not contain this section; they conclude Mark's Gospel with verse eight. This is true of the early versions as well: Syriac, Coptic, Armenian, and Georgian. The early church fathers, Clement, Origen, Cyprian, and Cyril of Jerusalem had no knowledge of anything beyond verse eight. There is little wonder that the noted manuscript authority Dr. Westcott states, "the verses which follow [9-20] are no part of the original narrative but an appendage." Among other noted scholars of the same opinion are Tregelles, Tischendorf, Griesbach, Metzger, and Comfort, to mention just a few.

Adding weight to this evidence of the Greek manuscripts, versions and church fathers are the church historian Eusebius and the Bible translator, Jerome. Eusebius wrote that the longer ending was not in the "accurate copies," for "at this point [verse 8] the end of the Gospel according to Mark is determined in nearly all the copies of the Gospel according to Mark." In addition, Jerome, writing about 407 C.E. said, "nearly all Greek MSS have not got this passage."

The vocabulary and style of Mark 16:9-20 vary so drastically from the Gospel of Mark that it scarcely seems possible that Mark himself wrote those verses. Mark's style is plain, direct; his paragraphs are short, and the transitions are simple. However, in this ending, there is well-arranged succession of statements, each of them having proper introductory expressions.

Then there is the consideration of the vocabulary of Mark. Verses 9 through 20 contain words that do not appear elsewhere in Mark's Gospel, and some that do not appear in any of the Gospels, and some still that do not appear in the whole of the Greek New Testament. Verses 9 through 20 contain 163 Greek words, of which, 19 words, 2 phrases do not occur elsewhere in the Gospel of Mark. Looking at it another way, in these 12 verses there are 109 different words, and, of these, 11 words and 2 phrases are exclusive to these 12 verses. Moreover, the doctrinal thesis of Joseph Hug showed that when compared with the vocabulary of the other Gospels, the Apostolic Fathers, and the apocryphal literature, you have 12 verses in "an advanced state of tradition." The note at the end of Metzger's The Text of the New

Testament, where I found a summary of Hug's thesis, states:

> The vocabulary suggests that the composition of the ending is appropriately located at the end of the first century or in the middle of the second century. Those who were responsible for adding the verses were intent, not only to supply a suitable ending for the Second Gospel, but also to provide missionary instruction to a Christian Hellenistic community that participated in charismatic activities... (Metzger 1964, 1968, 1992, 297)

The content of these verses also remove them from being considered as original. There is nothing within the whole of the New Testament, which would support the contention in verse 18 that the disciples of Christ were able to drink poison, having no harm come to them. In addition, within this spurious text, you have eleven apostles refusing to believe the testimony of two disciples whom Jesus had come across on the way and to whom he made himself known. However, when the two disciples found the eleven, their reaction was quite different, stating, "The Lord has risen indeed, and has appeared to Simon!" Luke 24:13-35

In summary, Mark 16:9-20 **(1)** is not found in two of the oldest and most highly regarded Greek manuscripts as well as others. **(2)** They are also not found in many of the oldest versions. **(3)** The early church fathers had no knowledge of anything beyond verse eight. **(4)** Such ancient scholars as Eusebius and Jerome marked them spurious. **(5)** The style of these verses is utterly different from that of Mark. **(6)** The vocabulary used in these verses is different from that of Mark. **(7)** Verse 8 does not transition well with verse 9, jumping from the women disciples to Jesus' resurrection appearance. Jesus does not need to appear because Mark ended with the announcement that he had. We only want that because the other Gospels give us an appearance. So we expect it. **(8)** The very content of these verses contradicts the facts and the rest of the Greek New Testament. With textual scholarship, being very well aware of Mark's abrupt style of writing, and abrupt ending to his Gospel does not seem out of place. Eusebius and Jerome, as well as this writer, agree.

Mark 16:17-18 New King James Version (NKJV)

[17] And these signs will follow those who believe: In My name **(1)** they will cast out demons; **(2)** they will speak with new tongues;**(3)** [18] they will take up serpents; and if they drink anything deadly, it will by no means hurt them;**(4)** they will lay hands on the sick, and they will recover."

Is this really, what the Bible teaches?

While Paul was bitten by a poisonous snake and survived, we never find anyone in the New Testament going out to find poisonous snakes, for the purpose of handling them in a religious service. To the contrary, Paul quickly shook off the poisonous snake that had attached itself to his hand. One must ask, 'what purpose would religious snake handling have?' All of the gifts that were bestowed on the first century Christians had a practical purpose. The number one purpose was to evidence to the Jews that the Israelite nation was no longer the way to God, faith in Jesus Christ was.

As for Tongues, They Will Cease

Some may argue that the evidence does not give one any idea of when the gift of tongues was to end. However, they would be mistaken in this case. There are three lines of evidence that present the fact that the gift of tongues would die out shortly after the death of the last apostle, which was the apostle John, who died about 98-100 C.E. **First**, the gift of tongues was always passed on to the person, only by an apostle: either by laying his hands on this one, or at least being present. (Acts 2:4, 14, 17; 10:44-46; 19:6; see also Acts 8:14-18.)**Second**, 1 Corinthians 13:8 informed the Corinthian reader specifically that this gift would "cease." In short, the Greek word for cease [*pausontai*], means to 'peter out,' or 'to die out,' not to be brought to a halt. We will deal with *pausontai* more extensively in a moment. **Third**, both one and two are exactly what happened when we look at the history of this gift of tongues. M'Clintock and Strong's *Cyclopaedia* (Vol. VI, p. 320) say that it is "an uncontested statement that during the first hundred years after the death of the apostles we hear little or nothing of the working of miracles by the early Christians." Therefore, following their passing off the scene and after those who in that way had obtained the gift of tongues breathed their last breath; the gift of tongues should have died out with these ones. (Elwell, 2001, 1207-8) This analysis concurs with the intention of those gifts as acknowledged at Hebrews 2:2-4.

Daniel B. Wallace in his *Greek Grammar Beyond the Basics* helps us to better comprehend how we are to understand *pausontai* of 1 Corinthians 13:8:

> If the voice of the verb here is significant, then Paul is saying either that tongues will cut

themselves off (direct middle) or, more likely, cease of their own accord, i.e., 'die out' without an intervening agent (indirect middle). It may be significant with reference to prophecy and knowledge, Paul used a different verb ([katargeo]) and out it in the passive voice. In vv 9-10, the argument continues: 'for we *know* in part and we *prophecy* in part; but when the perfect comes, the partial shall be done away with [katargethesontai].' Here again, Paul uses the same passive verb he had used with prophecy and knowledge and he speaks of the verbal counterpart to the nominal 'prophecy' and 'knowledge.' Yet he does not speak about *tongues* being done away 'when the perfect comes.' The implication *may* be that tongues were to have 'died out' on their own *before* the perfect comes. (Wallace 1996, 442)

Speaking in Tongues and Today's Christianity

The gift of tongues "in the NT has three functions: to show the progress of the gift of the Spirit to the various people groups in the book of Acts in a salvation-history context, as a way of revealing the content of the NT revelation, and as a means of communicating cross-linguistically."[63] The apostle Paul made it abundantly clear that the interpretation must be clear and understood for the benefit of all, not the glorification of

---

[63] Chad Brand, "Tongues, Gift Of", in *Holman Illustrated Bible Dictionary*, ed. Charles Draper, Archie England, Steve Bond et al., 1606 (Nashville, TN: Holman Bible Publishers, 2003).

one. (1 Corinthians 14:26-33) Paul gave a warning: "So with yourselves, if with your tongue you utter speech that is not intelligible, how will anyone know what is said? For you will be speaking into the air." 1 Corinthians 14:9

It is true that many of the early Christians received this gift of tongues by way of Holy Spirit, which did *not* bring forth speech that was incomprehensible or untranslatable nonsense. In accord with Paul's advice, the Holy Spirit made available speech that brought about an outcome in the gospel being "preached in all creation under heaven."—Colossians 1:23.

The church has been attempting with great vigor, to fulfill, Jesus Christ's command of "the gospel must first be proclaimed to all nations." (Mark 13:10) The same as was the case in the first-century, all nations are required to take notice of the message of the ransom death, resurrection, and ascension of Christ. This is achievable for the reason that God's Word has now been translated into over 2,300 languages. The unchanged Spirit that instilled the first Christians to speak in tongues is now sustaining the immense and extraordinary commission of the present-day church. 2 Timothy 1:13

Final Thoughts

Indeed, no writer wishes to be arrogantly dogmatic about a belief, an understanding of Scripture that could be overturned or adjusted before his eyes, as he grows in knowledge and understanding. The evidence seems to say that the gift of tongues was given to some in the infant Christian congregation to establish it as the new way to God, to give witness to the mighty acts of God that include the ransom sacrifice of Christ, his resurrection and ascension, and to communicate rapidly to those who spoke other languages.

These abilities were only established by the presence or lying on of hands by the apostles. This coincides with 1 Corinthians 13:8 and the history of these phenomena. Our Greek word for "cease" means that the gift of tongues was to 'die out' over time as the last of those who had received this gift passed off the scene of this earth. This is established by the historical fact that the second century saw just that being evidenced. Today, the Christian is moved by Spirit to speak with his heart and mind, defending and establishing the gospel, and destroying false doctrines, snatching some back from the fire. It is these things, which will give credence to the words of the modern-day Christian congregation: "God is really among you." – 1 Corinthians 14:24-25

APPENDIX B Is Snake Handling Biblical?

Edward D. Andrews

Snake handling or serpent handling[64] is a religious ritual in a small number of Pentecostal churches in the U.S., usually characterized as rural and part of the Holiness movement. The practice began in the early 20th century in Appalachia, and plays only a small part in the church service. Practitioners believe serpent-handling dates to antiquity and quote the Gospel of Mark and the Gospel of Luke to support the practice:

Mark 16:17-18 New King James Version (NKJV)[65]

[17] And these signs will follow those who believe: In My name they will cast out demons; they will speak with new tongues; [18] **they will take up serpents**; and if they drink anything deadly, it will by no means hurt them; they will lay hands on the sick, and they will recover."

Luke 10:19 King James Version (KJV)

[19] Behold, I give unto you **power to tread on serpents** and scorpions, and over all the power of the enemy: and nothing shall by any means hurt you.

Another passage from the New Testament used to support snake handlers' belief is Acts 28:1-6, which relates

---

[64] http://en.wikipedia.org/wiki/Snake_handling

[65] We are using the King James Version throughout this chapter, because that is the only translation the charismatic snake-handlers will use. Therefore, we want you, the reader, to know what their preferred translation says.

that Paul was bitten by a venomous viper and suffered no harm. (More on this below)

Founders of Snake Handling

George Went Hensley preaching in 1947 outside a Hamilton County, Tennessee courthouse in which a snake-handling minister was on trial (from Taking Up Serpents: Snake Handlers of Eastern Kentucky by David L. Kimbrough)

George Went Hensley (1880–1955) introduced snake-handling practices into the Church of God Holiness, about 1910.[66] He later resigned his ministry and started the first holiness movement church to require snake handling as evidence of salvation.[67] Sister-churches later sprang up throughout the Appalachian region.[68]

Snake Handlers Today and Practices

As in the early days, worshipers are still encouraged to lay hands on the sick, speak in tongues,[69] provide

---

[66] Encyclopedia of American Religions gives the year as 1909; the Encyclopedia of Religion in the South gives it as 1913.

[67] Anderson, Robert Mapes (1979). *Vision of the Disinherited: The Making of American Pentecostalism*. New York, New York; Oxford: Oxford University Press. p. 263.

Hood, Jr., Ralph W.; Williamson, W. Paul (2008). *Them That Believe: The Power and the Meaning of the Christian Serpent-Handling Tradition*. Berkeley and Los Angeles, California: University of California Press. pp. xiv, 37, 38.

[68] David L. Kimbrough (February 2002). *Taking up serpents: snake handlers of eastern Kentucky*. Mercer University Press. pp. xiv, 37–51.

[69] See APPENDIX A: Is Speaking in Tongues a Biblical Teaching?

testimony of miracles, and occasionally consume poisons such as strychnine.[70] Gathering mainly in homes and converted buildings, snake handlers generally adhere to strict dress codes such as uncut hair, ankle-length dresses, and no cosmetics for women; and short hair and long-sleeved shirts for men. Most snake handlers preach against any use of tobacco or alcohol.

Most religious snake handlers are still found in the Appalachian Mountains and other parts of the southeastern United States, especially in Alabama, Georgia, Kentucky, North Carolina, Tennessee, West Virginia, and Ohio. However, they are gaining greater recognition due to news broadcasts, movies, and books about the non-denominational movement.

In 2001, about 40 small churches practiced snake handling, most of them considered holiness-Pentecostals or charismatics. In 2004, there were four snake-handling congregations in the provinces of Alberta and British Columbia, Canada. Like their predecessors, today's snake handlers believe in a strict and literal interpretation of the Bible, and most Church of God with Signs Following churches are non-denominational, believing that denominations are human-made and carry the Mark of the Beast. Worshipers attend services several nights a week, where if the Holy Spirit "intervenes," services can last up to five hours, the minimum is usually ninety minutes.

---

[70] Dennis Covington, *Salvation on Sand Mountain: Snake Handling and Redemption in Southern Appalachia* (Reading, MA.: Addison-Wesley, 1995).

Risks of Snake Handling

Some of the leaders in these churches have been bitten numerous times, as indicated by their distorted extremities. Hensley himself, the founder of modern snake handling in the Appalachian Mountains, died of snakebite in 1955.[71] In 1998, snake-handling evangelist John Wayne "Punkin" Brown died after being bitten by a timber rattlesnake at the Rock House Holiness Church in rural northeastern Alabama[72] although members of his family contend that his death was probably due to a heart attack. Brown's wife had died three years earlier after being bitten in Kentucky. Another snake handler died in 2006 at a church in Kentucky.[73] In 2012, Pentecostal Pastor Mack Wolford died of a rattlesnake bite sustained while officiating at an outdoor service in West Virginia, as did his father in 1983.[74]

Herpetologists have opined that the risk of fatal bites is significantly reduced by the familiarity of the snakes with humans, and by the poor health of snakes that are insufficiently fed and watered.[75]

---

[71] Brown, Joi. "Snake Handling in the Pentecostal Church: The Precedent Set by George Hensley". Virginia Tech. Archived from the original on 2005-07-18. Retrieved 2014-01-13.

[72] Custody of 'snake-bite orphans' split between grandparents". CNN. 1999-02-12. Retrieved 2014-01-13.

[73] Woman fatally bitten by snake in church". USA Today. Associated Press. 2006-11-08. Retrieved 2014-01-13.

[74] Duin, Julia (2012-05-30). "Serpent-handling pastor profiled earlier in Washington Post dies from rattlesnake bite". Washington Post. Retrieved 2014-01-13.

[75] John Burnett (2013-10-18). "Serpent Experts Try To Demystify Pentecostal Snake Handling". National Public Radio.

Does not Mark 16:17, 18 (NKJ) show that 'snake handling' would be a sign that one is a believer?

Mark 16:17-18 New King James Version (NKJV)

¹⁷ And these signs will follow those who believe: In My name they will cast out demons; they will speak with new tongues; ¹⁸ **they will take up serpents**; and if they drink anything deadly, it will by no means hurt them; they will lay hands on the sick, and they will recover."

Before offering our reasons why Mark 16:9-20 are not a part of the original manuscript of Mark, we will see what John Macarthur says,

16:9–20 The external evidence strongly suggests that these verses were not originally part of Mark's Gospel. While the majority of Greek manuscripts contain these verses, the earliest and most reliable do not. A shorter ending also existed, but it is not included in the text. Further, some that include the passage note that it was missing from older Greek manuscripts, while others have scribal marks indicating the passage was considered spurious. The fourth-century church fathers Eusebius and Jerome noted that almost all Greek manuscripts available to them lacked verses 9–20. The internal evidence from this passage also weighs heavily against Mark's authorship. The transition between verses 8 and 9 is abrupt and awkward. The Greek particle translated "now" that begins verse 9 implies continuity with the preceding narrative. What follows, however, does not continue the story of the women referred to in verse 8, but describes Christ's appearance to Mary Magdalene (cf. John

20:11–18). The masculine participle in verse 9 expects "he" as its antecedent, yet the subject of verse 8 is the women. Although she had just been mentioned three times (v. 1; 15:40, 47), verse 9 introduces Mary Magdalene as if for the first time. Further, if Mark wrote verse 9, it is strange that he would only now note that Jesus had cast seven demons out of her. The angel spoke of Jesus' appearing to His followers in Galilee, yet the appearances described in verses 9–20 are all in the Jerusalem area. Finally, the presence in these verses of a significant number of Greek words used nowhere else in Mark argues that Mark did not write them. Verses 9–20 represent an early (they were known to the second-century fathers Irenaeus, Tatian, and, possibly, Justin Martyr) attempt (known to the second-century fathers Irenaeus, Tatian, and, possibly, Justin Martyr) to complete Mark's Gospel. While for the most part summarizing truths taught elsewhere in Scripture, verses 9–20 should always be compared with the rest of Scripture, and no doctrines should be formulated based solely on them. Since, in spite of all these considerations of the likely unreliability of this section, it is possible to be wrong on the issue, it is good to consider the meaning of this passage and leave it in the text, just as with John 7:53–8:11.[76]

Now we will offer our arguments, First, there is the telling fact that two of the oldest and most highly

---

[76] MacArthur, John (2005-05-09). *The MacArthur Bible Commentary* (Kindle Locations 43226-43242). Thomas Nelson. Kindle Edition.

respected Bible manuscripts, the Vaticanus 03 and the Sinaiticus 01, do not contain this section; they conclude Mark's Gospel with verse eight. This is true of the early versions as well: Syriac, Coptic, Armenian, and Georgian. The early church fathers, Clement, Origen, Cyprian, and Cyril of Jerusalem had no knowledge of anything beyond verse eight. There is little wonder that the noted manuscript authority Dr. Westcott states, "the verses which follow [9-20] are no part of the original narrative but an appendage." Among other noted scholars of the same opinion are Tregelles, Tischendorf, Griesbach, Metzger, and Comfort, to mention just a few.

Adding weight to this evidence of the Greek manuscripts, versions and church fathers are the church historian Eusebius and the Bible translator Jerome. Eusebius wrote that the longer ending was not in the "accurate copies," for "at this point [verse 8] the end of the Gospel according to Mark is determined in nearly all the copies of the Gospel according to Mark." In addition, Jerome, writing about 407 C.E. said, "nearly no Greek MSS have got this passage."

The vocabulary and style of Mark 16:9-20 vary so drastically from the Gospel of Mark that it scarcely seems possible that Mark himself wrote those verses. Mark's style is plain, direct; his paragraphs are short and the transitions are simple. However, in this ending, there is well-arranged succession of statements, each of them having proper introductory expressions.

Then there is the consideration of the vocabulary of Mark. Verses 9 through 20 contain words that do not appear elsewhere in Mark's Gospel, and some that do not appear in any of the Gospels, and some still that do not appear in the whole of the Greek New Testament. Verses 9 through 20 contain 163 Greek words, of which,

19 words, 2 phrases do not occur elsewhere in the Gospel of Mark. Looking at it another way, in these 12 verses there are 109 different words, and, of these, 11 words and 2 phrases are exclusive to these 12 verses.

Moreover, the doctrinal thesis of Joseph Hug showed that when compared with the vocabulary of the other Gospels, the Apostolic Fathers, and the apocryphal literature, you have 12 verses in "an advanced state of tradition." The note at the end of Metzger's The Text of the New Testament, where I found a summary of Hug's thesis, states:

The vocabulary suggests that the composition of the ending is appropriately located at the end of the first century or in the middle of the second century. Those who were responsible for adding the verses were intent, not only to supply a suitable ending for the Second Gospel, but also to provide missionary instruction to a Christian Hellenistic community that participated in charismatic activities... (Metzger 1964, 1968, 1992, 297)

The content of these verses also removes them from being considered as original. There is nothing within the whole of the New Testament, which would support the contention in verse 18 that the disciples of Christ were able to drink poison, having no harm come to them. In addition, within this spurious text, you have eleven apostles refusing to believe the testimony of two disciples whom Jesus had come across on the way and to whom he made himself known. However, when the two disciples found the eleven, their reaction was quite different, stating, "The Lord has risen indeed, and has appeared to Simon!" – Luke 24:13-35

In summary, Mark 16:9-20 **(1)** is not found in two of the oldest and most highly regarded Greek manuscripts as well as others. **(2)** They are also not found in many of the oldest versions. **(3)** The early church fathers had no knowledge of anything beyond verse eight. **(4)** Such ancient scholars as Eusebius and Jerome marked them spurious. **(5)** The style of these verses is utterly different from that of Mark. **(6)** The vocabulary used in these verses is different from that of Mark. **(7)** Verse 8 does not transition well with verse 9, jumping from the women disciples to Jesus' resurrection appearance. Jesus does not need to appear because Mark ended with the announcement that he had. We only want that because the other Gospels give us an appearance. Therefore, we expect it. **(8)** The very content of these verses contradicts the facts and the rest of the Greek New Testament. With textual scholarship, being very well aware of Mark's abrupt style of writing, and abrupt ending to his Gospel does not seem out of place. Eusebius and Jerome, as well as this writer, agree.

Mark 16:17-18 New King James Version (NKJV)

17 And these signs will follow those who believe: In My name **(1)** they will cast out demons; **(2)** they will speak with new tongues; **(3)** 18 they will take up serpents; and if they drink anything deadly, it will by no means hurt them; **(4)** they will lay hands on the sick, and they will recover."

Is This Really, What the Bible Teaches?

While Paul was bitten by a poisonous snake and survived, we never find anyone in the New Testament going out to find poisonous snakes, for the purpose of handling them in a religious service. To the contrary, Paul quickly shook off the poisonous snake that had attached itself to his hand. One must ask, 'what purpose would religious snake handling have?' All of the gifts that were bestowed on the first century Christians had a practical purpose. The number one purpose was to evidence to the Jews that the Israelite nation was no longer the way to God, faith in Jesus Christ was.

"Thou Shall Not Tempt the Lord"

1 John 4:8 in the King James Version reads, "He that loveth not knoweth not God; for God is love." "Symptoms of a venomous snakebite include pain and swelling followed by nausea, vomiting, and weakness. These signs usually emerge within 30 to 60 minutes of the bite, but may also be delayed for several hours."[77] Does it seem like a loving God, who would expect his followers, purposely to inflict pain, suffering and possibly death on themselves?

There is a far greater difference of a God, who expects his followers to be faithful unto death, as opposed to violating Scripture; contrasted with one, who expects his followers needlessly to demonstrate their faith by handling poisonous snakes that can inflict pain and even death. This is especially true, when God can read their heart and mind, and knows whether they are faithful, and would be faithful in a life-threatening situation. Moreover, Christians, who die or suffer pain for their faith, are usually the result of an enemy of God inflicting it on them.

Now, recall the words of Satan to Jesus, "If thou be the Son of God, cast thyself down: for it is written, He shall give his angels charge concerning thee: and in their hands they shall bear thee up, lest at any time thou dash thy foot against a stone." Jesus responded, "It is written again, Thou shalt not tempt the Lord thy God." (Matt 7:6-7) When a minister asks you to test God, or prove

---

[77] http://www.webmd.com/women/news/20020802/dont-suck-snakebite

your faith, by risking your life in snake-handing, would not Jesus' very words apply? If you test God, are not you demonstrating a lack of faith? Are you not forcing him to carry out your will and purposes of protecting you, upon being bit?

What About Luke 10:19?

Luke 10:19 King James Version (KJV)

19 Behold, I give unto you **power to tread on serpents** and scorpions, and over all the power of the enemy: and **nothing shall by any means hurt you**.

If this was meant to be taken literally; then, all of those pastors mentioned above, and far more, would have never suffered in pain, until they died. In addition, no true Christian ever bitten by a poisonous snake or scorpion would have felt the pain of the poison from that bite.

These words have frequently been quoted in close connection with Mark 16:18. A literal interpretation is then given to both passages. At times, Acts 28:3 is also cited. However, Paul did not deliberately pick up a venomous snake nor did he step on it. As to the authenticity of Mark 16 (16:9–20) see N.T.C. on Mark, pp. 682–687. In the passage now under discussion, namely, Luke 10:19, the figurative explanation is almost certainly the correct one. Note the following:

> a. Jesus often made use of figurative language, though such language was frequently interpreted literally (Matt. 16:6–12; Luke 8:52, 53; John 2:19–21; 3:3, 4; 4:13–15; 6:51, 52; 11:11–13, etc.).

> b. In the immediately preceding passage (verse 18) the Lord had used symbolical

language when he spoke of seeing Satan falling from heaven like lightning.

c. If elsewhere Satan is called "dragon" and "serpent" (Rev. 12:9; 20:2), why should it be strange if also here in Luke 10:19 the domain of the prince of evil is called that of snakes and scorpions? Is it not Satan's intention to *poison* the minds of men and to impart the *sting* of death to all who oppose him?

d. There is no record of any *literal* fulfilment of this statement.

e. The true interpretation is also supported by the explanatory expression "(I have given you authority over) ... *all the power of the enemy.*" For explanation, see Rom. 16:20, "The God of peace will soon crush Satan under your feet."

As to the promise, "And nothing will in any way hurt you," see John 10:27, 28; Rom. 8:28–39.

In addition, there is no record of snake handling until the modern day charismatic church. If this was meant to be practiced, we would have historical records over an 1800-year period, but we do not. Moreover, the apostle Paul was able to resurrect people from the dead, and he did survive many life-threatening moments, yet he never purposely risked his life, testing or demonstrating his faith, or testing God. (1 Timothy 5:23; 2 Timothy 4:13) Paul did not look for opportunities to resurrect people, to show he had the ability to do so.

What are Christians actually asked to do with their bodies?

Romans 12:1 King James Version (KJV)

1 I beseech you therefore, brethren, by the mercies of God, that ye present your bodies a living sacrifice, holy, acceptable unto God, which is your reasonable service.

2 Corinthians 13:5 King James Version (KJV)

⁵ Examine yourselves, whether ye be in the faith; prove your own selves. Know ye not your own selves, how that Jesus Christ is in you, except ye be reprobates?

No, we do not risk our lives to 'examine whether we are in the faith,' we rather look at our new Christian personality, making sure that we live by Scripture, evidencing our true Christianity by doing as James said, "faith without works is dead." If we need to test something, it is our doctrinal positions: are they biblical, or just the word of man.

Other Books in This Series

The SECOND COMING of CHRIST

What Is Hell?

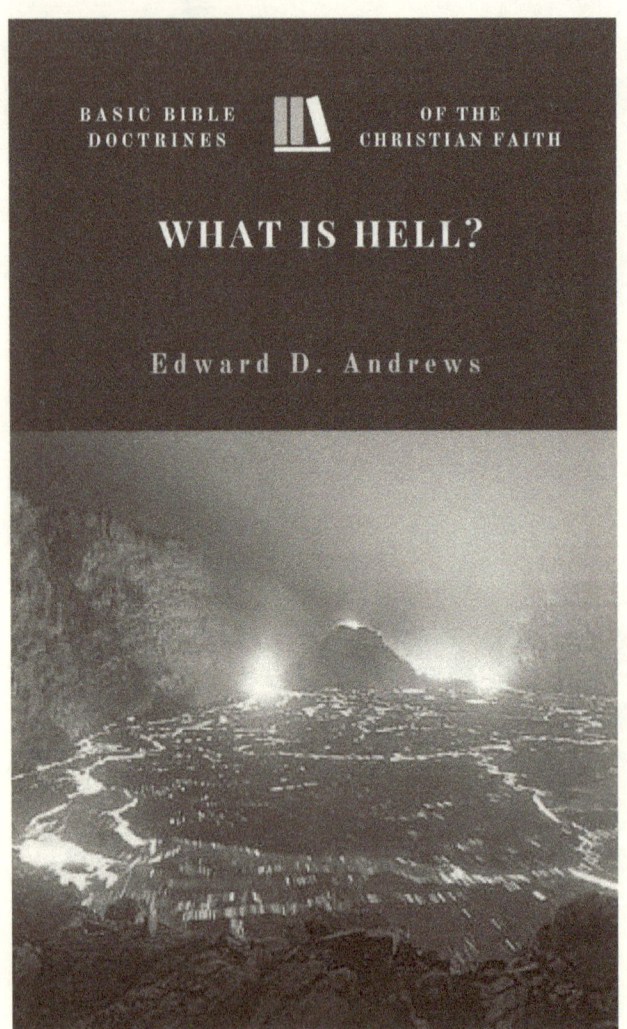

Where are the Dead?

Explaining the Doctrine of Man

Bibliography

Akin, Daniel L., David P. Nelson, and Jr. Peter R. Schemm. *A Theology for the Church.* Nashville: B & H Publishing, 2007.

Anders, Max. *Holman New Testament Commentary: vol. 8, Galatians, Ephesians, Philippians, Colossians.* Nashville, TN: Broadman & Holman Publishers, 1999.

Anders, Max, and Trent Butler. *Holman Old Testament Commentary: Isaiah.* Nashiville, TN: B&H Publishing, 2002.

Bercot, David W. *A Dictionary of Early Christian Beliefs.* Peabody: Hendrickson, 1998.

Blomberg, Craig. *The New American Commentary: Matthew.* Nashville, TN: Broadman & Holman Publishers, 1992.

Boa, Kenneth, and Kruidenier. *Holman New Testament Commentary: Romans.* Nashville: Broadman & Holman, 2000.

Borchert, Gerald L. *The New American Commentary: John 1-11 .* Nashville, TN: Broadman & Holman Publishers, 2001.

Borchert, Gerald L. *The New American Commentary vol. 25B, John 12–21.* Nashville: Broadman & Holman Publishers, 2002.

Brand, Chad, Charles Draper, and England Archie. *Holman Illustrated Bible Dictionary: Revised, Updated and Expanded.* Nashville, TN: Holman, 2003.

Bromiley, Geoffrey W., and Gerhard Friedrich. *Theological Dictionary of the New Testament, ed. Gerhard Kittel, vol. 4.* Grand Rapids, MI: Eerdmans, 1964-.

Campbell, Alexander. *The Christian System (6th ed.;.* Cincinnati: Standard, 1850.

Easley, Kendell H. *Holman New Testament Commentary, vol. 12, Revelation.* (Nashville, TN: Broadman & Holman Publishers, 1998.

Easton, M. G. *Easton's Bible Dictionary.* Oak Harbor, WA: Logos Research Systems, 1996, c1897.

Elwell, Walter A. *Evangelical Dictionary of Theology (Second Edition).* Grand Rapids: Baker Academic, 2001.

Elwell, Walter A, and Philip Wesley Comfort. *Tyndale Bible Dictionary.* Wheaton, Ill: Tyndale House Publishers, 2001.

Enns, Paul P. *The Moody Handbook of Theology.* Chicago: Moody Press, 1997.

Erickson, Milliard J. *Christian Theology (Third Edition).* Grand Rapids, MI: Baker Academic, 2013.

Ferguson, Everett. *Baptism in the Early Church: History, Theology, and Liturgy in the First Five Centuries .* Grand Rapids, MI: Eerdmans, 2009.

Gangel, Kenneth O. *Holman New Testament Commentary: Acts.* Nashville, TN: Broadman & Holman Publishers, 1998.

Gangel, Kenneth O. *Holman New Testament Commentary, vol. 4, John .* Nashville, TN: Broadman & Holman Publishers, 2000.

Geisler, Norman L. *SYSTEMATIC THEOLOGY: God and Creation (Vol. 2)*. Minneapolis: Baker Publishing Group, 2003.

George, Timothy. *The New American Commentary: Galatians* . Nashville, TN: Broadman & Holman Publishers, 2001.

Green, Joel B, Scot McKnight, and Howard Marshall. *Dictionary of Jesus and the Gospels*. Downers Grove, IL: InterVarsity Press, 1992.

Gruden, Wayne. *Are Miraculous Gifts for Today?: 4 Views (Counterpoints: Bible and Theology)*. Grand Rapids: Zondervan, 2011.

Larson, Knute. *Holman New Testament Commentary, vol. 9, I & II Thessalonians, I & II Timothy, Titus, Philemon*. Nashville, TN: Broadman & Holman Publishers, 2000.

Lea, Thomas D. *Holman New Testament Commentary: Vol. 10, Hebrews, James*. Nashville, TN: Broadman & Holman Publishers, 1999.

Lea, Thomas D., and Hayne P. Griffin. *The New American Commentary, vol. 34, 1, 2 Timothy, Titus*. Nashville: Broadman & Holman Publishers, 1992.

Martin, D Michael. *The New American Commentary 33 1, 2 Thessalonians* . Nashville, TN: Broadman & Holman, 2001, c1995 .

Mcgrath, Alister E. *Christian Theology: An Introduction*. Malden, MA: Blackwell, 2001.

McReynolds, Paul R. *Word Study: Greek-English*. Carol Stream: Tyndale House Publishers, 1999.

Melick, Richard R. *The New American Commentary: Philippians, Colossians, Philemon, electronic ed., Logos Library System*. Nashville: Broadman & Holman Publishers, 2001.

Microsoft. *Encarta ® World English Dictionary*. Redmond: Microsoft Corporation, 1998-2010.

Mirriam-Webster, Inc. *Mirriam-Webster's Collegiate Dictionary. Eleventh Edition*. Springfield: Mirriam-Webster, Inc., 2003.

Mounce, Robert H. *The New American Commentary: Vol. 27 Romans*. Nashville, TN: Broadman & Holman Publishers, 2001.

Mounce, William D. *Mounce's Complete Expository Dictionary of Old & New Testament Words*. Grand Rapids, MI: Zondervan, 2006.

Polhill, John B. *The New American Commentary 26: Acts*. Nashville: Broadman & Holman Publishers, 2001.

Pratt Jr, Richard L. *Holman New Testament Commentary: I & II Corinthians, vol. 7*. Nashville: Broadman & Holman Publishers, 2000.

Richardson, Kurt. *The New American Commentary Vol. 36 James*. Nashville: Broadman & Holman Publishers, 1997.

Robertson, A.T. *Word Pictures in the New Testament*. Oak Harbor, MI: Logos Research Systems, 1933, 1997.

Rooker, Mark F. *Leviticus: The New American Commentary*. Nashville: Broadman & Holman, 2001.

Ryrie, Charles C. *Basic Theology*. Chicago, IL: Moody Press, 1999.

Smyth, Herbert. *Greek Grammar for Colleges* . New York: American Book Company, 1916.

Sweeney, Z. T. *The Spirit and the Word (: , n.d.), 121–26.* Nashville: Gospel Advocate, 2005.

Swindoll, Charles R, and Roy B. Zuck. *Understanding Christian Theology.* Nashville, TN: Thomas Nelson Publishers, 2003.

Towns, Elmer L. *Theology for Today.* Belmont: Wadsworth Group, 2002.

Vine, W E. *Vine's Expository Dictionary of Old and New Testament Words.* Nashville: Thomas Nelson, 1996.

Wallace, Daniel. *Greek Grammar Beyond the Basics.* Grad Rapids: Zondervan, 1996.

Walls, David, and Max Anders. *Holan New Testament Commentary I & II Peter, I, II & III John, Jude.* Nashville: Broadman & Holman Publishers, 1999.

—. *Holman New Testament Commentary: I & II Peter, I, II & III John, Jude.* Nashville: Broadman & Holman Publishers, 1996.

Weber, Stuart K. *Holman New Testament Commentary, vol. 1, Matthew.* Nashville, TN: Broadman & Holman Publishers, 2000.

Wuest, Kenneth S. *Wuest's Word Studies from the Greek New Testament: For the English Reader.* Grand Rapids: Eerdmans, 1997, c1984.

Zodhiates, Spiros. *The Complete Word Study Dictionary: New Testament.* Chattanooga: AMG Publishers, 2000, c1992, c1993.

www.ingramcontent.com/pod-product-compliance
Lightning Source LLC
Chambersburg PA
CBHW022358040426
42450CB00005B/243